George Chachis

CH2-8175

Iran at the End of the Century

Iran at the End of the Century

A Hegelian Forecast

Robert E. Looney
University of Santa Clara

Lexington Books
D.C. Heath and Company
Lexington, Massachusetts
Toronto

Library of Congress Cataloging in Publication Data

Looney, Robert E
  Iran at the end of the century.

  Bibliography: p.
  1. Iran—Economic conditions. I. Title.
HC475.L65   339′.0955   75-36895
ISBN 0-669-00405-7

Published simultaneously in Canada.

Printed in the United States of America.

International Standard Book Number: 0-669-00405-7

Library of Congress Catalog Card Number: 75-36895

To My Parents

Contents

List of Figures and Tables

Preface

The presence of immense oil resources in Iran has imposed upon the government the responsibility for capitalizing on those resources for the economic development of the country and concomitantly for the benefit of the people, not only for the present but for the future.

Since the beginning of Iran's oil boom,[1] the national income has increased rapidly, but a wide disparity still exists between the various classes and the various regions, indicating characteristic signs of economic backwardness. The lowest 10 percent of families in the income scale, for example, account for only 2.5 percent of the total consumption, whereas the highest 10 percent account for 32.5 percent.[2] Industry is largely concentrated in Tehran, where per capita income is 45 percent higher than in other large provincial cities and 70 percent higher than in small towns.[3] Modernization has not reached into every corner of Iran, nor is the resource base evenly divided. Considerable educational and cultural differences exist, and some areas either are inaccessible or have not yet been penetrated by efficient commercial transporation. As a result, the great majority of the Iranian population has not been incorporated into the purchasing power brackets needed to sustain the extensive and dynamic industry now manufacturing consumer durable goods. Furthermore, the rural zones, particularly in the agricultural-based west and south of the country, where half the population lives, show the lowest average family income.

In Iran, lower income is usually synonymous with households still producing only in the subsistence sector. High-income groups are in general urbanized and associated with modernized Western technologies and tastes. Therefore a duality of social structures largely coincides with the income distributional pattern. In short, a number of inconsistencies and conflicts between the governed and the monarchy have been built up as a result of the oil boom.

Thus success in creating an integrated national structure out of essentially different income and social groups must be one of the main factors characterizing and determining the country's progress in the next third of the century. The essence of this dramatic progress will be the struggle of emerging classes and social groups, each having its own particular goals and interests.

The outcome of that struggle will depend upon the steps taken by the government to resolve the problem, and this will depend upon the proficiency of the forecasts. Thus far government forecasts have not been successful, since they have not taken into account all the relevant factors.

It is the purpose of this book, therefore, to rectify this circumstance by organizing a framework for forecasting the economic future of Iran based both on Hegel's method and system and on other essential factors integral to the economy. We will also analyze the likely developments in the country and the probability of resolving the existing conflicts as well as describe the probable state of affairs stemming from this analytical process.

The name "Hegel" at once suggests the expression "dialectical logic." Hegel, of course, has a place in a long tradition of logic which began with Plato, left its high-water mark on Plotinus, Scotus, Erigena, Nicholas of Cusa and Fichte, and continued through Lotze, Ferrier, Bradley, Green, Bosanquet, McTaggart, Royce, and Collingwood. But Hegel's *Science of Logic* and his companion portion of the *Encyclopedia of the Philosophical Sciences* continue to stand out as the most systematic attempts to develop such a logic and to establish the relations between logic and reality.

In the area of economics, Marx attempted to develop Hegel's dialectical logic as the basis for long-run forecasts of economic growth.[4] Interestingly Marx, in spite of his ultradetailed analysis, was able to deal only with situations of growth growing out of growth; that is, if in a certain period a country can produce an excess capacity with respect to the current level of demand, then it can do likewise in the subsequent period, and then again and again forever (subject to the availability of natural resources). But that is not the way economies develop. Marx ignores the fact that the essence of growth is nothing but a passage from a level of output to another level of higher output, just as accelerated motion means the passage from one uniform motion to another such motion. The problem of forecasting long-run growth in an economy such as Iran's will therefore be solved when a model is developed that can represent analytically *only* this passage from one state to another.[5] A modification of form of Hegel's dialectical logic is developed here in a non-Marxian manner for precisely that purpose.

This book grew out of the author's disillusionment with the nature of long-run forecasts, since when they have been made, they have not incorporated institutional and cultural elements into the system in an explicit manner. The importance of these social and institutional factors in development economics has always been acknowledged by economists, yet their relevance has not been systematically examined. Most theories and the forecasts upon which they are based go only so far as to mention the customary list of cultural factors. For example, a large body of literature in recent years has been concerned with the growth of population, the progress of technology, and the accumulation of capital. Using these factors, an attempt is then made to analyze the similarity of these growth patterns with those observed in other nations at similar or higher levels of per capita income. But these patterns are in fact products of the country's culture and institutions, and any effort to extrapolate or alter them necessarily involves a commitment to some theory of the forces responsible for changes in economies over time.

This book seeks, therefore, to make a long-run forecast of the Iranian economy by integrating the modern analytical tools of economics with the theory of historical change stemming from the work of Hegel.

The literature on the future contains very little analysis of this type.[6] It should be expanded because progress in this direction would yield results not only of scientific interest but also of great practical value which will enable countries to plan their economies more rationally.

Given its scope, the book should be of particular interest to students of the Iranian economy. Others more interested in areas such as Hegel's philosophy, the problems of long-run forecasting, world economic conditions in the latter part of the twentieth century, and Marxian economics will also find the book informative.

Notes

1. The country's oil revenues have continually increased since the early 1950s. The current boom, of course, began with the OPEC price increases of late 1973. For an excellent account of the country's oil sector, see Feridun Fesharaki, *Development of the Iranian Oil Industry—International and Domestic Aspects* (New York: Praeger Publishers, 1976).

2. Bank Markazi Iran, Economic Statistics Department, "Urban Household Budget Survey in Iran," Tehran, 1968; Montek S. Ahluwalia, "Income Inequality: Some Dimensions of the Problem," in Hollis Chenery, et al., *Redistribution with Growth* (London: Oxford University Press, 1974), pp. 3–37.

3. E. Naraghi, "Regional Studies in Iran," in *Multidisciplinary Aspects of Regional Development* (Paris: OECD, 1969).

4. Cf. Alexander Balinky, *Marx's Economics* (Lexington, Mass.: D.C. Heath, Lexington Books, 1970), chapter 2.

5. Nicholas Georgescu-Roegen, "Economic Growth and Its Representation by Models," *Atlantic Economic Journal,* **4:** 1–8, 1976.

6. For a recent evaluation of Hegel's method and system, cf. Alasdir MacIntyre, ed., *Hegel: A Collection of Critical Essays* (Garden City, N.Y. Doubleday & Co., 1972). For a recent interpretation of one aspect of Hegel's system, see A. O. Hirschman, "On Hegel, Imperialism, and Structural Stagnation," *Journal of Development Economics,* **3:** 1–8, 1976.

Acknowledgments

The author is indebted to more individuals than can be conveniently identified here. However, for their stimulating discussions and ideas, I would like especially to thank Robert Davenport and Peter Duncan of Stanford Research Institute; Sheldon Simon, Max Borlin, and Hal Fischer of the Battelle Memorial Institute; Peter Gajewski of Louis Berger International; Momoud Fajdar and Ahmed Kooros of Bank Markazi Iran; Constantin Mejloumian and Firouz Vakil of the Iranian Plan Organization; Daniel Dick and Mario Belotti of the University of Santa Clara; and Amhed Sabouchi of La Verne College. Lorie Bazan of the University of Santa Clara gave invaluable insights into the Hegelian system, as did M. Laina Farhat into the history and culture of Iran. Jake Virts, Robert Miller, and Glenn Knapp, also of the University of Santa Clara, designed the computer programs used in the study. Special thanks are owing to Christine Tapley for her invaluable assistance in structuring and editing the manuscript. For her patience in typing the rough drafts and final manuscript, I would like to thank my wife, Anne.

1 Introduction

As the art of forecasting gains increasing ground in the realm of academic thought, the significance of projecting the unthinkable and predicting the unpredictable becomes quite apparent among those engaged in any sort of national development planning. Still, there is a basic conflict between those economists who resort to simple extrapolation of historical patterns and those who attempt to build models that allow for major changes such as innovations or other adjustments in the economy that differ from past patterns. Hardly any serious author has failed to take account of the dichotomy of the two methods.[1]

The Shah himself recognized the significance of forecasts. In a speech[2] delivered in May 1975, he observed that the key to the country's success in achieving high rates of growth was that its officials managed to keep the country a few steps ahead of current developments. He warned that it was not enough to be in pace with the times. To survive, the country should try to be several steps ahead of its neighbors.

In recent years the government of Iran has assumed the major responsibility for the country's economic development and growth. Along with this responsibility has come an increased awareness among the country's planners of the interrelation of different sectors of the economy and of the need for coordination of policies that had previously been examined only in terms of their direct impact on individual sectors— agriculture, industry, and so on.

In attempting to develop more realistic identification of the mechanisms at work in their economy, Iranian economists have utilized a number of widely known models:[3] a set of national income and product accounts, along with input-output tables, and associated linear programming models of the well-known optimization type.[4] More recently, experiments with long-run forecasts of an econometric type pioneered by Tibergen[5] have been developed in the Plan Organization[6] (the official planning agency). The purpose of these models was to determine the likely constraints the economy will face, the best allocation of oil revenues to overcome those constraints, and the timing of development projects for maximizing rates of national income growth. But the inaccuracy of this method of planning in Iran has been so great that all forecasts of the economy to date have been useless in terms of increasing the rate of growth of national income or of improving its distribution.

The Iranian public sector is not poor in resources (because of oil

1

revenues), but it is slow and complicated in procedure, uncoordinated in operation, and frequently inefficient in the execution of its programs. Government administration seems to be organized in a way more appropriate to the past, when economic development was altogether unplanned. Consequently, the task of coordinating the policy of development must be carefully evaluated in economic terms; it cannot be left to partial arrangements, emergencies, or the impromptu solutions of politicians or so-called experts. The government, although it has realized that its problems of growth have become more complex and difficult to solve, has not sufficiently applied itself to formulating an integrated development policy expressed in attainable quantitative objectives that anyone could understand. There is little public discussion of the alternative courses of action open to the government.[7] There is certainly talk of planning, sometimes dealing with one sector of the economy, sometimes with a region. But it appears to be no more than a physical planning of projects without any clear economic content. A nationwide concept of the country's long-run development potential is lacking, as are adequate studies and forecasts of long-run eventualities on which to base government policy.

If Iran has in the past carried out a reasonably effective combination of policies, the policies have not always been well coordinated. The policies—in view of population growth, of uncertainties as to the continued rate of expansion in oil exports, and of the new and complex issues ariring from growth itself and from changing social and political aspirations among the people—need to be updated and in some cases thoroughly revised. For example, to move in the direction of a sustained growth rate of about 12 percent annually—perhaps the minimum rate necessary to absorb an expanding young population into productive employment—agricultural and industrial growth will have to be more coordinated than in the past.

Government, particularly the Plan Organization, must face the issues and work out the necessary planning machinery to ensure optimum utilization of Iran's many positive trends and experiences in development. A mere continuation of the policies of the past is bound to fail in spite of both the successful overall growth rates since the mid-1960s and the current oil boom.

Notes

1. For a review of the current state of the arts, see Olaf Helmer, "An Agenda for Future Research," *Futures*, **6**: 3–14, 1975.

2. *Kayhan International*, May 3, 1975, p. 1.

3. For one of the first attempts in this area, see Reza Doroudian Shoja, "Econometric Models for the Fourth Plan," *Tahqiqat-e Eqtesadi*, **10:** 432–51, 1968.

4. See Max Borlin and Robert Looney, *The Battelle Linear Programming Model of the Iranian Economy* (Tehran: The Plan Organization, 1972).

5. J. Timbergen, *On the Theory of Economic Policy* (Amsterdam: North-Holland Publishing Co., 1952).

6. Firouz Vakil, "An Econometric Model for Iran," Bank Markazi Iran, *Bulletin*, **11:** 115–20, 1972; Firouz Vakil, "An Econometric Model for Iran: Estimated Structural Equations," Bank Markazi Iran, *Bulletin*, **12:** 633–55, 1973.

7. What critical discussion that does take place is mainly confined to Iranian students studying in Europe or the United States. Cf. Bahman Nirumand, *Iran: The New Imperialism in Action* (New York: Monthly Review Press, 1969).

2

Economic Growth, 1950–1972

Introduction

Iran, with a long-standing tradition of monarchy extending over 2500 years, has for years been one of the most stable countries in the Middle East. But economic development did not begin significantly until the closing years of the nineteenth century during the latter years of the rule of the Qajar dynasty. Since that time, however, economic and social change has taken place at an accelerated pace, although growth was interrupted by the political and economic dislocation following World War I. After the war, national unity and law and order were restored by the intervention of Reza Khan, leader of the Russian-trained Cossack regiment, who in 1925 assumed the monarchy as Reza Shah Pahlavi.[1]

Since the establishment of the Pahlavi reign in the mid-1920s, Iran has pursued a remarkably consistent development strategy, which has essentially followed the lines first defined by Reza Shah, that is, to modernize the economy as rapidly as its resources would permit. In practice this has meant that industrialization, self-sufficiency, and integration of the national economy have been stressed.

In examining the modern economic history of Iran, we have divided the country's history into what was essentially a preindustrialization phase extending from the end of World War II to 1962, with the economy specializing in oil and agriculture; a second phase from 1962 to 1968, which was a transitional period beginning with the initiation of the Shah's White Revolution (Appendix A); and a third phase from 1968 to 1972, a period of rapid growth within a stable external environment. The oil boom years (since 1973) forms a final phase. Since data on the major macroeconomic aggregates—consumption, investment, and so on—of the Iranian economy were not compiled until 1959, we use this date as the beginning for the analysis of the modern phase of the country's development.

A Profile of Change: 1959–1972

For almost a decade and a half (from the latter 1950s to the early 1970s) Iran maintained an outstanding record of sustained economic growth and balance-of-payments stability. The average rate of GNP growth was 9.2

percent in real terms (Table 2–1), while in current prices the rate was 11.6 percent, indicating the degree of price stability obtained during this period (Table 2–2). This record was matched by few other countries in the world, developed or developing, and it was closely linked with the country's increasing capability in conducting sound economic management. Iran began to be perceived by many economists as a country which, by initiating the White Revolution, has achieved the structural and sociopolitical conditions required for modernization in a stable environment. The country's reputation for financial prudence was greatly enhanced in the early 1960s when the government instituted a successful stabilization program, undertaken when the nation's balance-of-payments position began to weaken and thereby demonstrating a willingness and capacity to take corrective measures to put the economy back on a course on noninflationary growth.

In addition to its overall economic growth, per capita real income also increased, in spite of a high rate of population growth of 2.75 percent per annum.

Private Consumption and Income Distribution

To obtain an idea of the changes in the standard of living of the people as a whole, we use as a proxy the average per capita consumption expenditure for the private sector. Several trends stand out.

(1) Total public and private consumption expenditures as a percentage of GDP remained stable at about 81 percent in constant prices, while in current prices they averaged 82 percent; but they declined substantially from 82.2 percent in 1967 to 78.4 percent in 1972, indicating that the level of real savings increased in this period because of the slight upward trend in inflation. On the other hand, private consumption expenditure alone fell markedly in both constant and current prices from 73.7 percent of GNP in 1959 to 56.7 percent and 57.4 percent, respectively, in 1972.

(2) A general acceleration of the increase in the real standard of living occurred during 1962 to 1972, as evidenced by an increase in the average rate of growth of real per capita private consumption from 2.52 to 5.78 percent between 1962–1967 and 1967–1972.

(3) The difference between the rural and urban standards of living probably increased during the decade, since the agricultural sector was relatively stagnant. This is supported by the slow growth in rural consumption of 3.71 percent per annum between 1959 and 1971 as compared with 8.77 percent annual income for the urban areas.

(4) The relative economic position of some income groups changed. The statistical information available indicates that the rapid growth of the

Table 2–1
GDP, Total Consumption, Private Consumption, 1959–1972, Current Prices

Measure of Development	1959	1962	1967	1972	Annual Percent Rate of Growth			
					1959–62	1962–67	1967–72	1959–72
Population (Millions)	21.2	23.0	26.5	30.5	2.75	2.87	2.85	2.84
Gross National Product (Billion Rials)	283.9	340.4	556.5	1186.4	6.24	10.33	16.35	11.63
Per Capita GNP (Rials)	13,392	14,780	20,979	38,215	3.34	7.26	12.74	8.40
Total Consumption	239.5	287.7	457.5	929.7	6.30	9.72	15.24	11.00
Consumption per Capita	11,297	12,509	17,264	30,482	3.46	6.66	12.04	7.93
Private Consumption	209.2	252.3	371.6	680.5	6.44	8.05	12.86	9.50
Private Consumption per capita	9868	10,970	14,023	23,311	3.59	5.03	10.70	6.84
Total Consumption as a Percentage of Income (GNP)	84.4%	84.5%	82.2%	78.4%	—	—	—	—
Private Consumption as a Percentage of Income (GNP)	73.7%	74.1%	66.8%	57.4%	—	—	—	—

Source: Computed from data provided by Bank Markazi Iran.

Table 2–2
GDP, Total Consumption, Private Consumption, 1959–1972, 1959 Prices

Measure of Development	1959	1962	1967	1972	Annual Percent Rate of Growth			
					1959–62	1962–67	1967–72	1959–72
Gross National Product (Billion Rials)	283.9	324.2	513.8	889.0	4.52	9.65	11.59	9.18
Per Capita GNP (Rials)	13,392	14,091	19,389	29,148	1.72	6.58	8.50	6.17
Total Consumption	239.5	265.3	404.2	708.9	3.47	8.79	11.89	8.71
Consumption per Capita	11,297	11,535	15,253	23,243	0.70	5.75	8.79	5.71
Private Consumption	209.2	253.4	330.6	503.8	6.60	5.46	8.79	6.99
Private Consumption per Capita	9868	11,017	12,475	16,518	3.74	2.52	5.78	4.04
Total Consumption as a Percentage of Income (GNP)	84.4%	81.8%	78.7%	79.7%	—	—	—	—
Private Consumption as a Percentage of Income (GNP)	73.7%	78.2%	64.3%	56.7%	—	—	—	—

Source: Compiled from data provided by Bank Markazi Iran.

Iranian economy in the 1960s was relatively more beneficial to upper-income families, corresponding to the eighth, ninth, and tenth highest deciles of family income distribution. The 10 percent of the families with the lowest incomes apparently suffered a decrease in their share of total family income. It is this deterioration in the lowest income bracket that warrants the assertion that the income distribution has worsened.

A large part of the distributional problem is a reflection of the wide difference between rural and urban incomes, the latter averaging 6 to 7 times the former. A modern sector, consisting of the commercial farming system and the employed urban worker, coexists with a backward sector consisting of subsistence agricultural workers and the rural and urban unemployed. Social, economic, and cultural improvement is largely nonexistent in the backward sector and is impeded by the geographical configuration of the country, which reinforces the isolation of the rural sector and increases the cost of providing the infrastructure necessary to growth.

Government Consumption and Investment and Private Investment

Substantial variations occurred from 1959 to 1972 in government consumption and capital expenditures (Table 2–3).

1. Government consumption expenditures in constant prices rose nearly sevenfold from 30.3 billion rials in 1959 to 205.4 billion in 1972. The ratio of government consumption to GNP increased from 10.7 percent to 23.1 percent, the rate of increase accelerating rapidly after 1962.
2. Government investment expenditures in constant prices increased over fivefold from 20.8 billion rials in 1959 to 120.8 billion in 1972, and the ratio of government investment to GNP increased from 7.3 to 13.6 percent. Both patterns were similar in current prices. Government investment also grew at a faster rate in the second half of the period.
3. Private investment (Table 2–4) in constant prices increased from 31.9 billion rials in 1959 to 91.7 billion in 1972. The share of private investment to GNP, while increasing from 11.2 percent in 1959 to 11.3 percent in 1967, actually declined from the latter date to 10.3 percent in 1972.
4. The ratio of private investment to public investment declined substantially from 1.53 in 1959 to 0.76 in 1972. The 1972 figure was the result of a decline from 1962 when the ratio had risen to 1.68.

The above figures indicate that a major structural change took place

Table 2–3
Government Consumption and Investment, 1959–1972, 1959 Prices

Measure of Development	1959	1962	1967	1972	Annual Percent Rate of Growth			
					1959–62	1962–67	1967–72	1959–72
Government Consumption (Billion Rials)	30.3	31.9	73.6	205.4	1.73	18.20	22.78	15.86
Government Consumption per Capita (Rials)	1429	1387	2777	6.734	−0.99	14.89	19.38	12.66
Government Consumption as a Percentage of GNP	10.7%	9.8%	14.3%	23.1%	—	—	—	—
Government Investment	20.8	18.4	55.1	120.8	−4.00	24.5	17.0	14.49
Government Investment per Capita	981	800	2079	3961	−6.57	21.05	13.76	11.33
Government Investment as a Percentage of GNP	7.3%	5.7%	10.7%	13.6%	—	—	—	—

Source: Computed from data provided by Bank Markazi Iran.

Table 2–4
Comparison of Government and Private Expenditures, 1959 Prices

Measure of Development	1959	1962	1967	1972	Annual Percent Rate of Growth			
					1959–62	1962–67	1967–72	1959–72
Private Investment (Billion Rials)	31.9	31.0	58.0	91.7	–0.95	13.35	9.59	8.46
Private Investment per Capita (Rials)	1505	1348	2189	3006	–3.61	10.18	6.55	5.47
Private Investment as a Proportion of GNP	11.2%	9.6%	11.3%	10.3%	—	—	—	—
Private Investment ÷ Government Investment	1.53	1.68	1.05	0.76	3.17	–8.97	–6.26	–5.24
Private Consumption ÷ Government Consumption	6.90	7.94	4.49	2.46	4.79	–10.78	–11.34	–7.63
Private Expenditure ÷ Government Expenditure	4.72	5.65	3.02	1.83	6.18	–11.77	–9.53	–7.03

Source: Computed from data provided by Bank Markazi Iran.

during the last decade in the role of the public sector. Government investment and consumption both increased at about double the rate of their private counterparts. The increasing economic role of the public sector was made possible by extensive increases in goverment borrowing during the 1962–1967 period and by sharp increases in oil revenues thereafter.

The government's reliance on borrowing as a means of financing its increased rate of expenditures points to one of the most serious of the latent problems in Iran's economy, that is, the large difference between domestic savings and the amount of investment required to maintain a high rate of growth. This gap grew appreciably after 1959. Domestic savings financed less than 80 percent of gross investment in 1970, compared with 84 percent in 1959.

More significantly, government savings began to finance an increasingly small proportion of public investment amounting to only 30 percent in 1969, compared to nearly 50 percent in 1959. As a result of government expenditures outrunning revenues, the public sector's accounts deteriorated from a surplus in 1962 to a deficit of 51.8 billion rials in 7 years. The government's resort to external borrowing and deficit financing had, by 1968, reached inflationary proportions.

Clearly there was both the need and the room for higher levels of taxes in Iran. Fortunately, the basis of a dynamic direct tax system was well laid through the tax reform of 1968, although advantages and costs of the numerous concessions and tax incentives granted to corporations still needed careful reexamination. Before the tax reforms in the late 1960s, the government's revenue base was deficient in the area of indirect taxation; and not only new taxes, but a whole new administrative assessment and collection apparatus had to be created.[2]

Elements Contributing to Sustained Growth

Throughout much of the 1959–1972 period, sustained expansion seems to have been the result of the following conditions: (1) the maintenance of a high level of private domestic savings (as evidenced by the falling proportion of consumption in GNP) and the continued inflow of foreign private and public capital resulting from the acceleration in government borrowing from abroad; (2) the maintenance of a high level of investment in which the private sector (including the foreign private sector) remained willing to invest and reinvest in productive enterprises; (3) the development of institutional bases of confidence between the public and private sectors; (4) the control of inflation to a level consistent with stability necessary to maintain confidence in the economy on the part of both savers and investors; and (5) the absence of serious foreign exchange constraints to growth, which meant that the current balance-of-payments deficit remained manageable and the country could honor its foreign exchange obligations.

On the general level, the expansion of output was clearly a function of sustained private and public investment, and the relatively unconstrained availability of labor, enterprise, and technology were further contributors to the nation's rapid increase in income during this period.

The role of government after 1962 was both direct, in terms of public sector investment, and indirect, in terms of policies which affected private sector investments. The general economic objectives of Iranian leaders appear to have been:[3] (1) rapid growth, and (2) the degree of social progress compatible with rapid growth within a framework of political stability, which was not only an end in itself but a condition of economic and social progress. This strategy succeeded largely because the country's sociopolitical evolution supported both public policies and private responses and helped to maintain quiet in the rural sector while facilitating faster socioeconomic mobility in an urbanizing society.

The Problem of Economic Dualism

Development during this period was characterized by the creation and growth of a modern (urbanized) sector, whose patterns of consumption, standards of living, and production techniques approached those of the developed countries.[4] Per capita incomes in the modern sector, already very high relative to the average Iranian level, continue to rise. Also, the number of people participating in this modern sector was increasing. The government, however, did not make a serious effort to spread evenly the fruits and the financial means of development by slowly lifting the standards of production and living of the larger part of the population. Rather, average income and productivity increased as a result of a swift transfer of a small but growing segment of the population from the traditional to the modern sector. This entailed the creation of a more unequal income distribution in which most new wealth was accruing to the already wealthy sector. Yet, as more people moved swiftly from the ranks of the small middle class to the ranks of the well-to-do, the ratio of rich to poor (at least of the very upper class to the poor) was growing rapidly.[5]

In the early 1960s, "modern sector" was almost synonymous with Tehran; it was an area where most modern industry was established, where a large service sector grew, where practically all corporations—even those which operated in the provinces—still had their headquarters. Iran's largest commercial bank, which has a comprehensive countrywide network, makes more than 70 percent of its loans to the Tehran province. However, locational policy underwent a sharp change in the latter 1960s. This was prompted by the government's belief that the marginal social cost of further growth of Tehran would soon rise sharply—essentially because of limited water supply—and by the government's desire to spread the process of development in provinces outside Tehran. The new policy had three aspects: (1) new manufacturing plants within a radius of 120 kilometers of Tehran were forbidden, and the ban was fairly strictly enforced; (2) large new public sector firms were created far from Tehran, that is, Tabriz, Isfahan, Arak, Ahwaz; and (3) the authorities actively and successfully used a series of special tax concessions and other fiscal inducements to attract private firms to these new areas of development.[6]

Therefore, although the basic development strategy emphasized the role of the modern sector, the remainder of the country was not neglected. In only a few years, the land tenure system was radically reformed, and the old semifeudal relationship of sharecropping peasants to large (often absentee) landowners was ended. Major literacy, health, and family planning campaigns were begun.

By 1973, however, Iranian society still remained hierarchical, with power anchored in individuals rather than in institutions. Though elite groups appeared to compete for power, the Shah managed to maintain a balance among them, making himself in effect the sole political arbiter. An able administrator with an international outlook, he leavened his absolute power with such concepts as decentralization, public participation in the means of production, and profit sharing. At the same time, he maintained his personal power base out of fear that factional rivalry would bring development to a standstill as it had in the early 1950s.

To summarize, by the early 1970s, two separate economic spheres of Iran were drifting apart, with rural areas stagnating and cities gaining, albeit not as rapidly as some of the statistics would have us believe. In the long run, it appeared that the gulf was to widen with dangerous political consequences; that is, many farmers would continue to migrate from the countryside to urban areas because of employment opportunities, which would thus deprive the agricultural sector of its best workers. Another matter of concern was the liberating impact, especially on women and children, of the move to the cities. The breakdown of traditional rural values and religious structures was becoming especially apparent among university students.

Government Expenditures on Services

Despite their increase, public services in many fields were still quite rudimentary in the late 1960s. For instance, little more than half of the primary-school-age population received any schooling, and in 1962 the literacy rate was less than 20 percent. The same situation existed in many other fields—communications, secondary and higher education, public health and sanitation, and above all general public administration, where services lagged well behind needs. Yet the increase in public services was actually much faster than the increase in expenditures, since Iran had used educated conscripts as teachers, health workers, and rural vocational teachers.

These "Revolutionary Corps" (Literacy Corps, Health Corps, Development Corps, and more recently on similar lines, the Women's Corps) allowed a rapid buildup of services at relatively low budgetary cost and contributed enormously to Iran's development by spreading new services even to the remote countryside. However, this was largely a once-and-for-all addition, in the sense that by the late 1960s the system had been well introduced and extended by drawing on an already existing number of qualified workers. Because of the increasing shortage of educated personnel, the government's attempt at maintaining the momentum of the 1960s began to involve a steep increase in costs (largely wages) involved in providing additional services. Furthermore, although the Revolutionary Corps had rendered and continued to provide extremely valuable services, they obviously had reached their limitations. Again, due to a shortage of trained staff, the Revolutionary Corps could supply only a relatively young, inexperienced, temporary staff. In addition, the financial needs of administration were also increased by the relatively high and rising incomes and opportunities provided by the private sector, particularly in the growing industrial centers of Isfahan and Tehran. The quality and volume of public services obviously could not be maintained, let alone increased, if the gap between private incomes and civil service pay rates continued to increase.

Role of the Private Sector

In addition to the importance of profit expectations, the level of private investment appears to have been related to (1) the general level of confidence in the economy and in the government's economic management and (2) the nature and degree of the incentives derived from the government's macroeconomic and sectoral policies.

The slow development of the government's policy toward the private sector stabilized the process of change in Iranian society and accelerated the process of economic growth because it allowed the government substantial freedom of action. However, this freedom would not have been associated with rapid growth in the absence of the growth of a mutual understanding between the private sector and the government. Reassurance came partly from experience as the private sector learned that the government would probably not intervene in the day-to-day activity of business and at the same time would establish a high tax rate on profits. Also the confidence of the private sector was not shaken by the rapid increase in government expenditures because the government allocated resources to investments that were in large part complementary to those in which private investments would likely occur. A further factor related to the growth of mutual understanding was the continued process of institutional development on the foundations that had been laid in the 1920s and 1930s. This process was vital to the achievement of rapid growth, in that the effectiveness of public/private sector relationships was dependent on the efficiency of the institutional framework. This did not mean the federal government alone; although its branches were certainly part of the network of institutions through which economic policy was implemented. It means that all the post-Reza Shah institutions played a part in the economic system, including (1) the federal government, (2) the public sector enterprises, and (3) the institutions of the financial system.

The choice of measures to finance public investment during the 1950s and 1960s was dictated in part by a low tax ratio, with oil revenues picking up much of the slack. But it was a reflection of the view widely held in high government circles that a higher tax ratio would imply an environment that was less conducive to private savings, investment, and reinvestment. Therefore the strategy for financing public investment was implicitly also a strategy for promoting private investment.

Throughout this period, government policy toward foreign investment was based on an informal code under which[7] (1) certain sectors of the economy were reserved to Iranian enterprise; (2) certain sectors of the economy (such as oil) were reserved for state enterprises; (3) foreign investment was to involve the establishment of new firms—and thus net investment; (4) foreign investment was particularly welcome if it was associated with the introduction of new technology; and (5) foreign investment was to result in the creation of new employment opportunities. The emphasis accorded to these several aspects of foreign investment policy varied somewhat over time, but their net effect was reflected both in the growth of foreign participation and in a substantial shift in the activities in which this investment took place.

Public and Private Expenditures: Summary

With these patterns in mind, two major questions can now be addressed: (1) how can we evaluate the underlying causes of the events and trends that have been described, and (2) what can be said about the implications of these trends, positively and negatively, for the future development of the Iranian economy?

The very rapid growth rates, as well as the decreasing role (in relative terms) of the private sector, are a direct result of both the rapid increases in the oil revenues and the institutional aspects associated with the introduction of these revenues into the economic and social mainstream. That oil revenues find their way to the economy via government institutions means that increases in government consumption, in government investment, and in the percentage share of each of the GNP are a function of the increases in such revenues. Were the oil revenues to begin to taper off, we would expect (at this stage of Iranian development) a decrease both in the rate of growth and in the share of government consumption to GNP as well as in government investment to GNP. Under such conditions, and because of the mixed (private and public) nature of Iran's economy, the country would have to rely on the private sector to stimulate growth. It is clear that the private sector is not in a position to pick up the slack.

It is also clear that in Iran, the recent period of very rapid growth associated with major structural changes has led to a worsening in the distribution of income. Unless specific policies are adopted to mitigate this trend, distribution of income will undoubtedly worsen in the foreseeable future. For example, the ratio of private urban consumption to private rural consumption on a per capita basis is bound to increase over the next 25 years. Indeed, a comparison of the rates of increase in the ratio of urban to rural consumption in 1959 and after indicates a large and steady increase in the annual rate of growth of this ratio (Table 2–5). Given that the rate of economic growth was much more rapid in the period after 1967, it is probable that there is within the present economic and social structure a positive correlation between vary rapid growth and worsening of the nation's distribution of income. Given that the Fifth Plan growth rates were projected to be above Fourth Plan growth rates, and that they have already (1975) been far overachieved, it seems evident that unless there are drastic policy changes, this intersectoral equity will worsen in the future.

Exports

Iran is the world's fourth largest producer of petroleum after Saudi Arabia, the U.S.S.R., and Kuwait; it accounts for approximately 10

Table 2-5
Urban-Rural Consumption Patterns, 1959-1971, 1959 Prices

Measure of Development	1959	1962	1967	1971	Annual Percent Rate of Growth			
					1959-62	1962-67	1967-71	1959-71
Total Consumption (Billion Rials)	106.9	122.9	187.2	293.0	4.76	8.78	11.85	8.77
Tehran	43.8	52.3	82.2	146.5	6.09	9.46	15.54	10.59
Large Cities	26.3	28.9	40.8	68.6	3.19	7.14	13.87	8.32
Other Cities	36.8	41.7	64.2	77.9	4.25	9.01	4.95	6.45
Rural Consumption	102.3	110.5	143.4	158.4	2.60	5.35	2.52	3.71
Urban Consumption as a Percentage of GNP	37.7%	37.9%	36.4%	37.6%	—	—	—	—
Rural Consumption as a Percentage of GNP	36.0%	34.1%	27.9%	20.4%	—	—	—	—
Urban Consumption ÷ Rural Consumption	1.045	1.112	1.305	1.850	2.09	3.25	9.12	4.87

Source: Compiled from data provided by Bank Markazi Iran.

percent of total world output. Over the past decade, oil production in the country has grown at an annual average rate of nearly 15 percent, reflecting an active program of exploration and development. Proven reserves have continued to increase, and Iranian reserves are estimated at about 66 billion barrels.

The export of petroleum and oil products far overshadows all transactions in the external trade sector of the Iranian economy. Total oil exports in the last few years (through a consortium of multinational oil companies and via joint ventures between the NIOC[8] and its foreign partners) have increased from about 1.3 billion barrels in 1969–1970 to about 21 billion barrels (nearly 300 million tons) in 1974–1975.[9]

Some 95 percent of petroleum exports is in crude, and more than three-quarters of crude exports go to Western Europe (41 percent) and Japan (35 percent). Exports of refined petroleum are largely destined for developing countries and Eastern Europe. The export of natural gas (mainly to the Soviet Union) is now the second most important source of export earnings—estimated to reach $190 million in 1974–1975.

The export performance of the economy during the period under consideration can be summarized as follows:

1. Total exports of goods and services have risen very rapidly, in line with GNP from 1962 to 1967.
2. Both oil exports and nonoil exports have had similar growth patterns in that the growth rates (annual) doubled in the 1967–1972 period, compared to 1962–1967.
3. Total exports as a percentage of GNP have increased from 12.8 percent in 1962 to 18.6 percent in 1972. This has more or less been matched by similar increase patterns in oil and nonoil exports during the same periods.
4. Of major interest to an oil-dependent economy is the ability of nonoil sectors to contribute to the growth of exports. The performance of the Iranian economy, particularly since 1962, suggests that nonoil exports have indeed kept up with the growth of oil exports, although in absolute terms they still constitute a relatively small proportion of Iran's foreign exchange earning capacity.
5. The ability of the oil and nonoil exports to cover imports declined from 1962 to 1967 and then climbed slightly from 1967 to 1972. Of importance to longer-run policy making in a country where a relatively fixed supply of natural resources is continually being depleted is the ability of the nonprimary resource exports to replace the primary resource as the main earner of foreign exchange. This means the eventual development of a comparative advantage on the international markets for certain manufactured items.

Imports

In a developing country such as Iran, imports have an especially important role to play in the development process. Modern technology and know-how as well as machinery and equipment have to be imported in relatively large quantities. The difference is only one of degree, of course, as can be seen from the fact that all the industrial countries except the United States, Britain, and Switzerland import more technology than they export, and Japan, Italy, France, Germany, and Sweden buy technology in multiples ranging from nearly 8 to over 2 of what they sell. The interchange of goods, including capital equipment, among the industrial countries, is always increasing and constitutes the major part of world trade. Iran can expect to be long dependent on imports while becoming increasingly interdependent with its trading partners.

Imports are classified in three component parts: consumer goods, intermediate goods, and capital goods. Sometimes the last two can be considered together as the inputs of investment, which is the heart of the development process. The import performance of the Iranian economy from 1959 to 1972 exhibits several distinctive features:

1. Total imports rose faster than the GNP did over the whole decade, rising from a 12.5 percent figure in 1962 to a 20.2 percent figure in 1972. The rise was fairly evenly distributed through 1962–1967 and 1967–1972.
2. Imports of capital and intermediate goods rose sharply in 1962–1972. The relative importance of this component in total imports indicates the sustained pattern of import replacement policies followed by Iran over that period.
3. Imports of consumer goods rose slowly during 1962–1967 and then accelerated in 1967–1972. Thus, the ratio of this category to GNP declined from 2.6 percent in 1962 to 2.0 percent in 1967 and then rose slightly to 2.1 percent in 1972.
4. Net imports of services rose at a phenomenal annual average of 41 percent over 1962–1972. This and the rapid rise of imports of capital and intermediate goods during those years were responsible for the increase in the ratio of total imports to GNP. Imports for the military and imports of skills are reflected in the net imports of services figures. In any case, this rise in imports indicates a growing confidence, over the period, in the ability of Iran to obtain foreign exchange.
5. The composition of imports shifted rather remarkably from 1962 to 1972: first, the share of consumer goods imports declined; second, the

share of capital and intermediate goods rose initially and then declined; and third, the share of net imports of services rose steadily.

From the point of view of a development strategy, the performance of imports from 1962 to 1972 suggests a very strong policy of import replacement in the consumer goods sector coupled with heavy protection policies destined to inhibit competitive imports. Thus, large imports of capital and intermediate goods were encouraged to set up import replacement industries, and imports of consumer goods were discouraged both to save scarce foreign exchange for investments and to protect the infant industries being set up behind tariff walls. The large increase in net imports of services reflects the importance of complementary technological skills required to operate factories in their infancy and to expand the nation's military capability. The figures reflect an increasing capacity to import, resulting from increasing export earnings mainly in the oil sector.

Production by Sector

Before World War II, Iran was still predominantly an agricultural society in terms of both the contribution of agriculture to GDP and the labor employed. In the last three decades it has changed the structure of its productive system to the extent that it is emerging from the status of a developing country to take its place in the foreseeable future among the developed industrial countries. The growth of oil has necessarily been the pivotal part of the change, but manufacturing has been becoming increasingly important in the economy, and its importance has accelerated (Table 2–6).

The following features are striking about the period.

(1) The growth of the industrial and mining sector was substantial throughout 1959 to 1972, accelerating somewhat in 1967 to 1972. The percentage contribution to GDP increased from 16.6 percent in 1962 to 19.8 percent in 1972, a substantial increase considering the very rapid rise in the contribution of the oil sector to GDP.

(2) The growth of the agricultural sector was substantially less than that of the other sectors, although the performance in 1962–1972 was a great improvement over that between 1959 and 1962. Thus, the contribution of agriculture to GDP decreased steadily from 27.7 percent in 1962 to 22.8 percent in 1967 and finally to 16 percent in 1972.

(3) The service sector remained stable as a percentage share of GDP at around 37.5 percent throughout the decade. Usually the service sector lags behind the industrial sector, if the strategy of economic development

Table 2–6
Production by Sector, 1959–1972

1959 Prices (Billion Rials)	1959	1962	1967	1972	Annual Percentage Rate of Growth			
					1959–62	1962–67	1967–72	1959–72
Agriculture	85.4	88.8	111.1	134.4	1.31	4.58	3.88	3.55
Oil	27.7	40.0	80.8	163.7	13.03	15.10	15.17	42.66
Manufacturing and Mining	30.9	41.5	72.5	138.1	10.33	11.8	13.76	12.21
Construction	13.3	14.1	24.9	35.0	1.97	12.05	7.05	7.85
Water-Electricity	1.1	2.2	8.9	21.1	25.99	32.25	18.84	25.5
Transportation and Communication	27.5	30.0	35.6	53.8	2.94	3.48	8.61	5.30
Banking	5.6	7.4	13.7	46.3	9.74	13.11	27.58	17.64
Domestic Trade	22.8	24.4	39.8	62.5	2.29	10.28	9.45	8.07
Housing Rent	15.5	19.1	27.7	39.9	7.21	7.72	7.57	7.54
Public Services	23.3	24.7	48.6	118.6	1.96	14.5	19.53	13.33
Private Services	13.0	14.2	21.6	42.8	2.99	8.75	14.66	9.60

Source: Computed from data provided by Bank Markazi Iran.

is aimed at promoting balanced growth. This is because the service sector operates on a derived demand basis with backward linkages from the strictly output-oriented agricultural and industrial sectors.

(4) The oil sector grew moderately during the 1962–1967 period and then had an annual average growth rate in value added of 24.1 percent for 1967–1972. Thus, as a percentage share of GDP, it was 18.3 percent in 1962, 19.9 percent in 1967, and 26.9 percent in 1972.

The structure of the economy has been affected for 20 years by the protective commercial system, with greater reliance on licensing than on import duties to restrict imports. Substitution of imports for consumption goods unintentionally militated against the production of capital goods. The concern about industrializing was universal after World War II, which undoubtedly accounted for worldwide neglect of agriculture. This influence may have been felt in Iran, and it may help to explain the decrease of investment in agriculture from the early 1950s onward.

Evaluation of Government Policy

Five fundamental issues are raised with regard to the public sector's increased levels of expenditure after 1962:

1. Was the magnitude of the changes that were sought in the real economy compatible with the capacity of the economy to make the necessary adjustment?
2. Was the time frame for this attempt reasonable?
3. Were the changes occurring in the economy consistent with the government's stated priorities?
4. Was the administrative and institutional framework of the public sector adequate to the task of implementing these priorities?
5. Was the government's development strategy conducive to a more equitable distribution of income?

None of these questions can be answered in a definitive way, but from the data presented above some tentative observations can be made.

For all its apparent success, the economic strategy of the 1960s suffered from two inherent deficiencies. (1) The public sector was not in a position to deal effectively with the problems of Iran's poor. These problems, judging from the apparently deteriorating trend of income distribution from 1960 to 1968, became more urgent with time. (2) Beginning in the middle 1960s, the government's emphasis was on the development of heavy industry through public investment. However, production proved inadequate to meet the domestic demand for basic industrial inputs, such as steel and electricity, which began to climb rapidly toward the end of the 1960s. The same problem began to appear in other sectors—including agriculture as well as the social sectors—which were not accorded an important place in the structure of public investment during most of the 1960s.

By the late 1960s, the government indicated awareness of these deficiencies and declared a willingness to correct them. The record shows that it has attempted to live up to this promise, at least in terms of expenditures. Whatever efforts were made, however, were made at the cost of contributing to an increasingly severe financial disequilibrium.

Domestic prices increased far more rapidly in the early 1970s than at any time since the early 1960s. The wholesale price index rose 5.6 percent during 1972; the average for 1972 was 5.7 percent higher than the average for 1971.[10] The balance-of-payments deficit on the nonoil current account rose from an average of around $1 billion in the late 1960s to $2.444 billion in 1972. The overall deficit of the consolidated public sector rose from $27.5 billion in 1967 to $56.2 billion in 1972.

Several external factors partially explain the deterioration in these key accounts: (1) some inflation was simply a result of the rapid increase in international prices; (2) the resource balance was affected by the deterioration of the terms of nonoil trade; and (3) part of the deficit in the balance-of-payments current account was attributable to an increase in interest payments on the public external debt. These payments resulted not so much from increasing indebtedness as from the deterioration in its terms (the interest cost plus amortization schedule).

All these factors notwithstanding, the major cause of disequilibrium was clearly that, in order to meet the targets of distributive justice and of a strong production base, the role of the public sector had to be vastly increased. Neither the administrative capacity nor the revenues accruing to the public sector were adequate to meet the magnitude of these tasks. The range of initiatives after 1962 (for example, the creation of the new institutions designed to improve the social situation in the country and the new massive investment in industry and agriculture) placed a tremendous strain on the capacity of the public sector. The magnitude of these changes, given the short time during which they were effected, would almost certainly have generated temporary distortions and fluctuations whenever they occurred. However, the distortions were compounded in Iran, in that the growth of domestic resources, while relatively rapid, still proved to be insufficient to meet quickly and steeply mounting claims on them. The government's priorities, therefore, had to be met to an increasing degree with borrowed resources.

The disequilibrium that was triggered mainly by the increase in the gap between public sector expenditures and revenues could probably not have been avoided, but it could have been somewhat attenuated through the curtailment of private sector demand. To a certain extent, there was a transfer of effective demand from the private to the public sector. Unfortunately, when private sector demand was reduced, it was investment that slowed down; trends in private consumption remained largely unaffected. Ideally, consumption by the upper-income groups, rather than investment by the private sector, should have decreased. Given the limited number of individuals in these income groups, this might not have been sufficient to maintain adequate levels of demand; neither would it have been feasible without drastic changes in Iran's social consensus.

Thus, the hidden flaw of the economic strategy of the post-White Revolution period was to have overlooked an obvious truth: to implement the rather revolutionary—and necessary—institutional changes and investment allocations which entailed a steep increase in public expenditures, an equally deep commitment had to be made to mobilize necessary revenues. Also, measures to increase revenues should have been taken early in the 1960s, since the time required for resource mobilization is normally longer than the time needed for implementing decisions leading to increased spending. The result was unprecedented growth in the public deficit and heavy recourse to internal and external borrowing. These deficits were the major forces behind the increasing inflationary pressures of the late 1960s and early 1970s. The external borrowing led to the rapid accumulation of outstanding external debt from a level of $661 million at the end of 1967 to $12.940 billion at the end of 1971.

Iran, therefore, continued up to 1976 to be threatened not from abroad but by problems at home, by the need to balance the desire for freedom and civil rights with rapid gains in the standard of living and material progress.

But the questions remain: Can a modern industrial state be run as a patriarchy? Do the means contradict the ultimate objective? What happens when more foreign experts are brought into the country and more young Iranians are sent abroad for their education? Will not the pressures to do away with the monarchy and introduce democratic institutions become irresistible? In other words, might the Shah be swung off the branch on which he is seated?

Conclusions

The outstanding variable of Iran's recent trends up to the Fifth Plan was the rapid real growth of the public sector. There can be little doubt that if the volume of expenditures of the public sector had not been attempted within an excessively short time, the disequilibrium of the early 1970s would have been much less severe, although external forces alone would probably have seen to it that prices rose and that the resource gap widened. Certainly, however, the magnitude of disequilibrium could have been greatly reduced.

Does this mean that the government should not have tried to address Iran's social and economic problems as vigorously as it did? There is no easy answer; but if the government had decided to abandon its commitments, Iran might well have a more stable economy today and might be facing less severe short-run problems. But the authorities hoped that by pressing ahead with the basic tasks, they would be able to initiate the creation of a stronger, less vulnerable, more diversified, and more equitable economic and social structure. Obviously, this effort has not entirely succeeded because in order to press ahead, Iran had to incur a heavy external debt and accept a high rate of inflation, and, as a result, the pattern of income distribution has worsened, not improved.

Notes

1. For an excellent account of Reza Shah, the founder of modern Iran, see Donald N. Wilber, *Reza Shah Pahlavi: The Resurrection and Reconstruction of Iran* (Hicksville, N.Y.: Exposition Press, 1975).

2. Cf. Nasrollah Vargar, "Economic Development in Iran and the Financing of the Gap in the Third Plan," *Middle Eastern Economic Papers* (March 4, 1964):45–63; also Robert Banks, *Financing Economic Development, Fiscal Policy for Emerging Countries* (Chicago: University of Chicago Press, 1968), p. 151. Vargar notes that in the early 1960s Iran's tax system was regressive and very poor in terms of yield, equity, simplicity, certainty of enforcement, and incentive. The collection procedure, according to him, was primitive, the administrative machinery obsolete, and corruption rampant (Vargar, "Economic Development in Iran," p. 119).

3. As outlined in the third and fourth Five-Year Plans. See Chapters 4 and 5 for a more detailed description of the objectives of these plans.

4. Described in detail in Jahangir Amuzegar and M. Ali Fekrat, *Iran: Economic Development under Dualistic Conditions* (Chicago: University of Chicago Press, 1971).

5. In 1972 the International Labor Office was asked by the Prime Minister of Iran to study the problems of employment in the country. The study as published [*Employment and Income Policies for Iran* (Geneva: International Labor Office, 1973)] alludes to the problem of income dis-

tribution, but does not document the trends during the 1960s. A working paper for the study prepared by Harry Oshima examines household budget surveys conducted by the Bank Markazi, and finds marked differentials in the income distribution, together with sufficient evidence to conclude that the distribution of income worsened during the 1960s.

6. As outlined in Robert E. Looney, "Industrial Decentralization in Iran," *University of Santa Clara Business Review*, 1974.

7. For a detailed summary, see Bank Markazi Iran, *Investor's Guide to Iran* (Tehran, 1969).

8. The National Iranian Oil Company.

9. Unless otherwise specified, data on oil production and exports are taken from *Oil and Gas Journal*, various issues.

10. Bank Markazi Iran, *Annual Report and Balance Sheet*, various issues.

3

Recent Growth: 1972 to Present

Introduction

Recent years have seen the pace of growth rapidly accelerate in Iran. By 1972 the rate of growth had risen to more than 14 percent per annum in real terms and increased perceptibly because of the steep upturn in oil revenues beginning in late 1973. Gross national product rose 34 percent in that year and 46 percent in 1974. These rates are unprecedented even by Iran's high standards of achievement. The dramatic increase in Iran's investment capacity made possible by the higher oil prices put the country in the enviable position of being able to have a wide range of discretion in terms of a series of radical changes in the structure of the economy. The revenues will permit a new strategy of industrial diversification, and perhaps even self-sufficiency in a number of areas. Obviously, miracles will not be created overnight. Rigorous and detailed planning will still be required to ensure the emergence of the optimum pattern of investment.

The Original Fifth Five-Year Plan

Even before the dramatic change in Iran's development prospects made possible by the OPEC price increases, the country had begun to orient its development strategy away from the achievement of high growth rates per se and more toward the establishment of the basis for self-sustained growth. The Shah, in his presentation of the Fifth Plan to Parliament, noted that the sustained economic growth and deep social changes in the previous 10 years preceding the White Revolution had elevated the nation to a position of leadership among the emerging nations. At the same time he warned that Iran's new stature had also placed the country in a position of moral responsibility to face more difficult and complex domestic issues.

He emphasized that the experience of other countries—whether developing or developed—indicated that rapid growth in national income had not necessarily resulted in a more equal distribution of that income. In order to ensure that the country made strides toward a more just distribution of income and wealth, the Shah proclaimed that the major orientation in the Fifth Plan was to increase social justice. As such, the plan was to be based on the principles of employment creation and

29

expanded social welfare expenditures; in particular it was to raise the living standards of the underprivileged classes.[1]

The stage for Iran's change in economic priorities was the Seventh Asian Regional Conference of the International Labor Organization, held in 1972 in Tehran. At that conference, Prime Minister Hoveyda articulated for the first time the government's changing position on poverty.

Basic Objectives of the Original Fifth Plan

Within the framework dictated by the Shah's philosophy, the basic aims of the original Fifth Plan were established in the following order of priority:[2]

1. To raise as much as possible the level of knowledge, culture, health, and welfare of the society
2. To attain a more equitable distribution of national income, with special attention to the rapidly increasing rise in the living standard and welfare of the underprivileged groups
3. To maintain the rapid and sustained rate of economic growth parallel with relative price stability and balance of payments
4. To provide productive employment in all regions of the country at a level that would absorb all the new workforce joining the labor market and substantially reduce concealed or seasonal unemployment
5. To operate fully the established production capacities built under the previous development plans, and to raise productivity and efficiency in the supply of goods and services in the public and private sectors
6. To improve the administrative order, in keeping with the lofty national aims and objectives, and to strengthen the country's defense capacity
7. To protect, improve, and revitalize the living environment
8. To increase Iran's share in international trade, particularly in manufactured goods

Overall Social and Economic Policies and Courses

To attain the general objectives of the plan, the projected investment was set at $24.5 billion (76.5 rials = $1). Given this sum, the planners anticipated that Iran's per capita income would increase to $2000 by 1978 (from $550 in 1972). A major aim in this direction was to reduce the annual rate of population growth by about half the present level (31 per 1000) by the end of 1991. In the shorter run, the goal of the Fifth Plan was to reduce the rate of population increase from the 31 per 1000 in 1972 to 26 per 1000 by the end of the plan (1977). It was anticipated that such a reduction would result in higher incomes and in improved living standards for the low-income classes in the urban centers.

To remedy some of the above-mentioned deficiencies, agriculture received special emphasis under the original version of the Fifth Plan. The plan target was to attain an annual increase in agricultural output of 5.5 percent and self-sufficiency in basic food items by the end of the plan period. Accordingly, agriculture was to receive a large share of government investment—102.6 billion rials (Table 3–1) intended to raise yields. Also, incentives—such as guaranteed minimum farm income prices for some products, increased agricultural credit, seeds, chemical fertilizers, and other basic requirements at low prices—were intended to stimulate

Table 3–1
Tran: Sectoral Revisions in the Fifth Five-Year Plan

Billion Rials, 1972 prices	Original Fifth-Plan Targets			Revised Fifth-Plan Targets		
	1972	1977	Average Annual Growth Rate	1972	1977	Average Annual Growth Rate
Agriculture	203.0 (16.6)	265.0 (12.6)	5.5	201.1 (18.1)	282.1 (8.0)	7.0
Oil	317.0 (25.9)	554.0 (26.3)	11.8	216.5 (19.5)	1712.0 (48.7)	51.5
Industry and Mining	240.5 (19.6)	489.0 (23.2)	15.0	274.4 (24.7)	566.0 (16.1)	18.0
Manufacturing and mining	165.0 (13.5)	336.0 (15.0)	15.3	—	—	—
Construction	56.0 (45.7)	103.0 (48.8)	13.0	—	—	—
Water	2.7 (0.2)	4.7 (0.2)	12.0	—	—	—
Power	16.8 (13.7)	45.3 (21.5)	22.0	—	—	—
Services	465.5 (38.0)	802.0 (38.0)	15.5	445.8 (40.1)	953.9 (27.1)	16.4
Gross Domestic Product	1226.0	2110.0	11.4	1110.8	3514.0	25.9

Source: Iran Trade and Industry Supplement No. 200, *TheFifth Plan* (Tehran, March 1973), p. 7; Kayhan Research Associates, *A Guide to Iran's Fifth Plan* (Tehran, 1975), p. 11.

( ) indicates percent GNP.

Between 1973 and 1975 the 1972 National Income Accounts for 1972 were revised. Between 1973 and 1975 the treatment of oil's contribution to GNP was changed so that the 1972 figures for oil are not comparable.

private sector investment in agriculture. These policies were expected not only to achieve greater efficiency in this sector but also to lessen the growing inequitable income distribution (since most of the lower-income households were in the rural areas).

The Revised Fifth Plan

Iran's Fifth Plan was originally approved by the Majles (Iranian Parliament) and the Senate early in 1973. But the subsequent sharp increases in oil prices and government revenues during 1973 and 1974 radically altered the plan's financial projections, enabling the government to undertake a wholesale upward revision of the plan's targets. The revised plan was submitted to the Parliament in the winter of 1974, and it called for a total fixed capital investment of 4699 billion rials (nearly $70 billion) between 1972 and 1977; it thus doubled the scope of the original 1973 version and increased the Fourth Plan (1968–1972) by sevenfold.

In revising the Fifth Plan, four basic considerations were of paramount significance to the planners. First, the shortage of domestic and foreign revenues, which had limited the size of previous development plans and influenced their order of priorities, was no longer a constraint. With the nearly certain prospects of continued rising oil revenues, the planners chose to aim at the maximum attainable growth in all sectors of the economy. Second, in setting the new priorities and growth targets, the planners remained mindful of such constraints as the country's inadequate supply of skilled workforce and technical personnel. The size of the plan was therefore intended to be commensurable with the country's domestic absorptive capacity, and allowances were made for potential new foreign investments. Third, an attempt was made to coordinate for the first time the process of five-year planning with the annual budget. Thus in theory the revised Fifth Plan expenditures were to closely parallel annual budgetary allocations. Finally, the new plan was to be set up in the context of a long-term 20-year perspective that presumably links it to the yet undrafted and unstructured Sixth and Seventh Plans.

Qualitative Objectives of the Revised Fifth Plan

Some revision was made in priorities in the revised version of the Fifth Plan, but basically the priorities were similar to those of the original version. In order of importance these objectives were:

1. To raise living standards of all social strata in the economy, and to

enhance social justice by providing equal economic, political, and cultural opportunities for all individuals and groups
2. To maintain a high and sustained rate of economic growth, consistent with relative price stability and a more equitable distribution of national income and welfare
3. To improve the quality and size of the country's active labor force to increase productivity
4. To preserve, rehabilitate, and improve the environment, especially in overpopulated areas
5. To upgrade the level of science, technology, and creativity
6. To preserve the country's cultural heritage and enhance the quality of life

Quantitative Allocations and Priorities

In allocating investment funds (Table 3–1) among the various sectors of the economy, the planners were motivated by three basic criteria. First, in the economic field, highest priority was assigned to industries in line with the nation's relatively abundant resources. Thus, the oil, gas, and petrochemical industries were singled out for the largest share of funds. Among other industries receiving relatively large sums were those manufacturing and mining activities such as steel, copper, and machine tools. Interior development, particularly ports, roads, and communications systems, were given top priority with the hope that investment in these areas would soon overcome existing (and in some cases anticipated) physical bottlenecks. Agriculture received relatively high allocations with the intention of allowing the country to achieve more and higher-quality foodstuffs, as well as greater raw material output for growing industries.

Second, in the area of social investments, housing, education, health, regional development, and environmental protection received the lion's share of funds. Third, public affairs allocations were geared toward giving the provinces greater voice in how public expenditures should be spent for urban and rural development, free education, a nationwide preventive health program, family planning, and expanded subsidies for essential needs of the lower-income groups.

Development under the Fifth Plan

In the first years of the plan (1973 to 1975), progressive legislation on housing, agrarian reform, and water use was introduced; a rural works program was expanded; and the concern with regional balance was translated into legislative action, as was also the objective of introducing a greater measure of control over price increases. Nevertheless, a number of problems remain: inflation, bottlenecks in transportation, skilled-labor shortages, and by 1976 a deficit in the government budget.

Inflation

Traditionally Iran has had relatively low rates of inflation—2 to 3 percent during most of the 1960s. However, owing to increased government expenditures made possible by the rapid inflow of oil revenues, the inflationary rate by 1975 had reached a rate of over 20 percent.[3]

In 1972–1973 the rate of budget expansion was 14 percent over that of the preceding year. The next year it grew by 50 percent. The year after that it expanded by 252 percent. This type of growth inevitably leads to increased money supply and liquidity, and therefore to an extended increase in general demand. Unless the rate of growth of the supply of goods escalates to accommodate the demand, inflation results. While supply coming from both domestic and foreign sources was increasing rapidly in Iran, it was not doing so at a speed approaching that of demand.

The authorities attempted to insulate the economy from the inflationary effects of the increase in oil revenues by:

1. An official foreign lending program
2. Freeing exchange controls
3. Freeing imports of gold and silver
4. The dismantling of import tariffs
5. A cut in government spending
6. Subsidy of consumer prices
7. Large-scale issues of state defense and housing bonds
8. Raising the commercial banks' deposit ratio with the Central Bank

Inflation by the end of 1974 was nevertheless running at a rate in excess of 25 percent. In view of the limitations to domestic production and the bottlenecks in the import system as is evidenced by inflationary increases from 1974 to 1975 (Table 3–2), inflation is likely to remain a continuing problem. Therefore, there is a very real possibility that the need to curb inflation will significantly slow the ambitious development plans.

The government itself has contributed significantly to inflation, especially in defense spending. In the summer of 1975, the revised Fifth Plan comprised a total budget of $122.8 billion, with $29.1 billion (23.7 percent) going to military and related expenditures. In addition to the dollar ex-

Table 3-2
Iran: Rate of Inflation First Half of 1975 Compared to First Half of 1974

	Percent Increase
GNP	150
Investment by Public Sector	30
Imported goods	110
Retail store sales volume	150
Savings and bank deposits	70
Bank System Lending to Private Sector	42
Locally manufactured automobiles	20
Tires	25
Lubricating oil	20
Antifreeze	75
Bricks	94
Tea	30
Textiles	25
Colored thread	240
Linseed oil	400

Source: Bank Markazi Iran, *Bulletin,* various issues.

penditure, defense was the more indirect cause of inflation, induced by the transfer of skilled workers to the military from the civilian establishment, which created a shortage of skilled labor and consequently rising salary rates of those in civilian pursuits.

Another factor in the inflationary mix is food. An increased money supply and an obvious improvement in the standard of living of the Iranian people have led to an increase in demand for both quantities and qualities of food, an increase which has led to an upward push in food prices. The government has been anxious to maintain stability among prices of various basic food commodities and has attempted with some success to do so by pouring $1 billion into the economy in the form of food price subsidies.

While the demand for food has been increasing at a rate approximating 10 percent per year, the domestically produced supply of these foodstuffs is growing at about half that rate. To supplement local production, the government has allowed imports of foodstuffs, and these have increased at such rates: grains, 200 percent; dairy products, 45 percent; and sugar, 50 percent. The excess of demand for food paired with the government's desire to maintain relatively stable and low prices has led to increased government spending in this area of the economy and has resulted in further inflationary pressures.

Not only have agricultural and other consumer goods been imported in great quantities, but the rates of importation of industrial and capital goods have been at very high levels to cope with demands in both public and private sectors. By 1975, the price-setting agency of the government, already in existence but relatively inactive during the first six months of 1975, was suddenly confronted with a flood of consumer, industrial, and other types of goods pouring into Iran. The agency found it impossible to keep up with the influx; consequently it was unable to assign appropriate prices to the goods, permitting them to reach the market at prices higher than they might otherwise have had, thus accelerating the price rate spiral.

To compound the problem of coping with the insatiable demand for goods, there was the matter of ports of entry and the interior distribution system, both of which were inadequate to their tasks. Import organizations and customs agencies, seaports and truck systems, together with warehouses and other distribution facilities, were all rapidly submerged by the oncoming tidal wave of goods. All these factors combined to frustrate the needs of the marketplace by adding costs to already expensive items and by delaying their arrival at purchase points and thus reducing the potential supply of goods needed to reduce inflationary pressures.

Workforce

The government has estimated that to achieve its economic goals would require many thousands of laborers and semiskilled workers; at the present time the shortage is about 700,000 workers. Further, requirements for skilled and educated people will accelerate far beyond the ability of the community to find them within its own ranks. A number of programs designed to attract foreign technicians have been developed, but the technicians have been low in efficiency of output and very high in cost. Added to the direct costs, in the form of high salaries and other financial inducements to encourage foreigners to come to Iran, has been an indirect cost. Foreigners have increased the strain on already heavily strained housing situations and thus have contributed to a runaway blackmarket in housing. The addition of relatively affluent people has compounded the gross demand and intensified competition for goods and services. In another sense, the rapid influx of foreign workers has led to difficulties that may have less obviously increased cost and prices. Cross-cultural difficulties between Iranians and foreigners have led to an increasing number of problems, and to losses in output and money, reflected in rapid rates of turnover and a reduction in the production and thus the output of the foreign workers.

As Iranian laborers experienced rising prices and observed the apparent financial affluence both of other Iranians and of foreigners, they believed they too should share in the new riches, and a variety of pressures came about which resulted in wage increases amounting to as much as 40 percent. Skilled labor pools diminished or disappeared even as the demand for skills was skyrocketing, and a skilled-labor black market soon developed in which workers moved from job to job, making whatever arrangements for remuneration seemed satisfactory to them and their new employers. These further increases in the totals being spent on income packages increased the potential for demand for products while giving no direct stimulus to expansion of supply.

Profiteering

In late 1973 to 1974 when inflation began, many managers escalated prices of their products in anticipation of further cost increases. The result was not only to accelerate inflation but to lead to profiteering. Soon an anti-profiteering sentiment arose which, along with the problems generated by the rate of inflation, led to a series of actions by the government that were intended not only to reduce the inflationary rate significantly but simultaneously to drive back prices to levels of earlier periods.

Budget Deficits

By 1976 much uncertainty had begun to surround Iran's ability to predict oil revenues effectively and budget them accordingly. Despite the problems of dwindling foreign exchange reserves, the government was not deterred from drawing up an overall budget (including the budgets of state-owned companies) that provides in the 1976–1977 fiscal year for a total expenditure of around 3,105,200 million rials ($45 billion), an increase of 27 percent over the budget for the previous year. The goal of the budget was to ensure stable prices in 1976. The forecast for revenues, however, shows a more modest rise of only about 15 percent to 2,056,800 million rials ($27.6 billion), and this leaves a deficit of $2.1 billion—even after allowing for foreign borrowing of $1.155 billion.

Whether the projected levels of expenditure can be attained, of course, remains to be seen. The government is clearly doing its best to minimize the growing public dissatisfaction concerning the setbacks in its development program by refusing to slow its target rates of growth. Ultimately, however, it must do so to provide relief for an economy that has been overextended beyond the limits of its resources.

Agriculture

The weak point in previous plans had been the agricultural sector, which has persistently failed to produce the growth demanded of it, in spite of considerable investment. This failure has led to changes in policy that followed the breakup of the big estates. In the early 1960s small-scale peasant farming based on the traditional Iranian village was encouraged. However, before the farms had been given a reasonable chance to succeed, policy was reversed and official finance and encouragement began to be centered on large-scale cooperatives and agrobusiness. In the interim, this change in agricultural policy has affected the confidence of the existing farming community, with the result that far from achieving the self-sufficiency in food, as postulated in the plan, agricultural imports have been escalating. For example, wheat purchases from abroad in 1975 were 2.1 million tons versus 600,000 tons in the previous year, and sugar imports were twice their 1974 level.

The success of the land reform program in changing the structure of farming from one of predominantly sharecropping relationships to one of owner operation has undoubtedly set the stage for the emergence of a modern, commercially oriented agricultural sector. It must be acknowledged, however, that little has been accomplished in the way of increasing the relative income of farmers. This will continue to be the case until farmers are given access to better knowledge, techniques, and inputs relative to their land. The requirements in terms of additional inputs (particularly irrigation water), extension services, credit, price guidance, and marketing facilities are large indeed and offer perhaps an even greater challenge than the reform already accomplished.

The agricultural crisis of recent years, therefore, seems in part to have its origins in demand and marketing in addition to supply. Production apparently has been increasing since the beginning of the Fifth Plan, and if estimates are correct, production is likely to surpass the historical trend of the last decade by a substantial margin. The marked increase in imports should probably be seen in light of the adverse implications of a poor harvest in 1974 and the fact that the government was unprepared to mobilize imports to fill the supply gap.

The fact remains, however, that the vast majority of Iran's peasants have been bypassed by rapid economic growth, and they barely participate in the market economy. In many ways, this is a consequence of policies that, except for agrarian reform, have focused on rapid increases in productivity and benefited a small number of large commercial farmers.

Mounting social pressures in the countryside and disappointing production performances in recent years may, however, indicate that a turning point has been reached in Iran's agricultural development and that the structural conditions may impose increasingly severe constraints to growth. For example, the more easily developable water resources have already been exploited; the extension of the cultivated area is becoming increasingly difficult; the further growth of output must increasingly depend on farmers who are less sophisticated than those in commercial agriculture; and the ecological conditions of the promising but so far virtually unused drier regions pose problems for which technological solutions have yet to be found.

Manufacturing

Despite the government's intention to reduce protection of domestic sales of manufactured goods, many problems still remained in the early 1970s. At that time, Iran's average tariff rates ranged from 351.8 percent for beverages to 11.7 percent for paper, but the rate was zero for a large number of items, including wheat, fertilizers, books, and sporting goods. In general, nonessential consumer goods had the highest rate of protection, whereas sectors producing mainly consumer goods, especially luxuries, had very high tariff rates.[4]

If we break the country's productive structure into twenty sectors, the six sectors ranked in order of the highest average tariff rates were beverages, tobacco, leather and footwear, wearing apparel, furniture, and food processing industries. Sectors that were primarily producers of intermediate goods generally had low ranks (that is, low tariff rates): mining, 19; petroleum, 15; paper and printing, 20; basic metals, 18; and machinery, 16. All had ranks of 15 or above. Although the average tariff rates in general conform to the structure observed in most countries (rates cascading from high levels in consumer to low or zero in capital goods), there were some exceptions. For instance, nonmetallic minerals (9), transport equipment (10), chemicals (12), rubber products (13), and metal products (14), which are essentially intermediate or capital goods producing sectors, had relatively high rates. These apparent exceptions to the general pattern of protection and price differentials are easily explained by the highly aggregative nature of these sectors. Many of them produce nonessential or luxury consumer goods or consumer durables, on which tariffs are quite high.

Another notable exception to the general tariff pattern is that in almost all sectors except tobacco and beverages, some items were subject to zero or nominal tariff rates because they were essential in either consumption (for example wheat, antibiotics, and books) or production (DDT, fertilizers, and tractors).

The most important implication of Iran's tariff structure is that the protection they afford from foreign competition allows some firms to earn comfortable profits, while others survive despite higher costs because of small-scale output or the use of more expensive local materials and components. There is clearly strong opposition among producers to any attempt by the government to force increased efficiency through lower protection.

Another important consequence of the bias toward domestic sales is that most of the investment decisions in Iran are still made almost exclusively in the context of the domestic market; exports are an incidental phenomenon. Profit expectations and realizations are often high in the protected domestic market, and there is naturally a great reluctance on the part of existing firms to make improvements so that export markets can be established; that is, given the internal and external price differentials, exports are simply not profitable.

In the short run, exports of manufactured goods could probably be stimulated through export subsidies. In the long run, however, a progressive reduction in protection is necessary and might bring some advantages in addition to gradually equalizing the profitability of exports and domestic sales: (1) plants could be designed and constructed for optimum size of the expected market (obviously, if that size requires exports because of the limitations of the domestic market, there would be less reluctance than at present to make that commitment); (2) greater specialization could occur within product groups. In addition to that increased specialization, lower rates of protection would enable producers to direct investments toward those products best suited to the availability of skills and resources in Iran. This restructuring of production is especially vital in light of the country's high rate of underemployment, particularly in the rural areas.

Several other deficiencies in the tariff structure need to be corrected. The high protection to producers of some intermediate inputs has generated high profits. These monopolistic returns have been an inducement to the final user to integrate backward. Not only has this process often been inefficient (owing to the small scale of output), but it has also prevented the economy from developing a network of specialized suppliers, each serving various industries. In the developed countries, the existence of efficient suppliers has been one of the principal sources of lower costs to firms using their products, and without these savings or inputs in Iran the growth of new industries has been retarded.

The effects of lower protection on the balance of payments cannot be determined with accuracy since a number of conflicting forces operate. Several general conclusions are possible, however. In the long run, lower protection would, through exposing firms to international competition, force the economy to operate more efficiently. A reduction in the rate of protection would also tend to increase the productivity of capital invested in the industrial sector, that is, by making it relatively more profitable to invest in areas oriented toward export markets rather than toward the domestic market. Since Iran has an abundance of labor, lower tariffs would result in more labor per unit of capital. Growth would thus be higher for a given savings rate. The additional production could go toward additional exports or import substitutes, both of which would improve the balance of payments. In the short run, however, lower protection would also make imports cheaper. Without the increase in oil revenues, lower protection could thus bring about an unacceptable deficit in the balance of payments. The country should therefore seriously consider lowering tariffs now rather than waiting until oil revenues level off or begin to decline.

Conclusions

Given political stability, the joint effect of large-scale inflows of oil reve- nues and determined economic and social development should result in the achievement of much of the Shah's promise that Iran will attain a standard of living akin to that prevailing in Western Europe. Per capita income could rise to as much as $2000 per year. Rapid demographic change, encouraged by the government, will result in more than 60 per- cent of the population living within the major cities. Rural peoples will be centralized in some 5000 large regional areas and environs, and the traditional village, of which there are some 50,000, will vanish. Although mechanization of agriculture will be introduced, there seems little pros- pect that plans for self-sufficiency in food will be achieved; Iran will become a food importer on an increasing scale. While industrial growth has characterized the economy over the past decade, the future for industries other than those based on hydrocarbons appears to be prob- lematical. Rising wage rates and the need to reduce tariffs on imported goods to restrain inflationary pressures will impede industrial progress to an increasing extent. It appears likely that the government will increas- ingly place emphasis on large-scale high-technology units to offset deficits in the manufacturing sector. Services are certain to replace industry as the main area of growth and employment creation.

The achievement of the Fifth Plan targets, and also the overall de- velopment prospects of the economy, depend not only on the govern- ment's ability to mobilize sufficient resources and disburse them, but also on the ability to coordinate social and economic policies. In particular, as the economy becomes more sophisticated, that is, as the direct links between the imports and outputs of different economic and social sectors become more widespread, so sectoral policies must be increasingly integrated.

The dramatic increase in Iran's investment capacity will create serious problems of investment strategy. The Fifth Plan has emphasized social and rural investment as a means of reducing the disparities generated by rapid economic growth, and the social aspect of development will continue to receive priority. The likely rise in investable resources is of such magnitude, however, that it is possible to think in terms of a radical change in the structure of the economy; that is, it is now possible for the country to implement a massive program of industrial diversification. At the same time, a large-scale investment program will make a skilled-labor shortage a distinct possibility. Therefore, it becomes important to choose industries that would make the largest contribution to the country's growth. The choice itself is not very difficult, for the pattern of specialization for Iran is indicated by its abundant reserves of oil, which most of the world will need in increasing amounts. However, detailed and rigorous planning will be required to ensure that the optimum pattern of industrialization emerges.

Notes

1. At the time of the revision of the Fifth Plan, the Shah noted that Iran was racing toward development far faster than was envisaged and that the country could attain these objectives. Cf. the Introduction to *Iran's Fifth Development Plan 1973–1978—Revised Summary* (Tehran: Plan and Budget Organization, May 1975).

2. *The Fifth Plan, Tehran: An Echo*, Iran Trade and Industry Publication, Supplement No. 200, March 1973, pp. 3–4.

3. Data are taken from the Bank Markazi Iran *Bulletin*, various issues.

4. Several excellent studies on Iran's tariff structure are available, and the data presented in the text is culled from these sources. See *Interregional Trade Projections, Effective Protection and Income Distribution—Volume II Effective Protection* (Bangkok: United Nations Economic Commission for Asia and the Far East), pp. 62–69; and Dragoslav Avramovic, "Industrialization of Iran: The Records, the Problems and the Prospects," *Tahqiqat-e Eqtesadi*, 1–13, Spring 1970.

4 Limitations of Existing Planning

Introduction

The terms "economic plan" and "economic planning" appeared in the Iranian political vocabulary for the first time[1] in the post-World War II period, and they have had wide circulation ever since. Out of the disruption caused by the war, the government leaders—under the prodding of younger intellectuals—drew up what was to be the country's first plan. This undertaking was also inspired in part by the policy of state intervention that emerged in the more developed Western countries[2] in response to what was anticipated to be a worldwide economic crisis similar to that experienced during the 1930s, and in part by what little was known in Iran at that time about Soviet planning.

In theory, planning in Iran has come to stand for the determination by the government (mainly through the Plan Organization, created in 1947 to implement the First Plan) of the degree and the manner in which the economy will make use of (1) its oil revenues (the exclusive source of funds for public development projects), (2) the market mechanism, and (3) its administrative system. The two mechanisms—market and administration—are seen by Iranian planners as instruments that can be used side by side to increase the potential contribution that the oil revenues can make to development. Therefore the real problem of planning in Iran is to organize that combination of the above three elements that will bring about the highest level of economic and social development over a given time period.[3]

In practice, however, while planning has been undertaken in Iran for almost three decades, it has not taken place within the framework of any definite political philosophy,[4] a necessary condition for achieving a consistent set of policies. In general economic plans have been conceived strictly from the economic side and have taken the existing political and social institutions for granted, rather than containing a blueprint for their orderly change. The economic system has continued to be a curious mixture of free enterprise and public intervention: the declared objective of the government is to encourage private enterprise, but its bureaucratic procedures and controls have stifled smaller enterprises. It is becoming increasingly apparent that the country's economic planning cannot proceed indefinitely in such a philosophic vacuum, particularly if planning is to acquire a long-run perspective. If Iran is to take advantage of the

43

potential that planning techniques have developed in Europe and the United States, the ultimate objectives of planning in the country must be clearly defined, and the social and political framework within which planning decisions are to be made must be outlined.[5]

The First Plan

Iran's First Plan (1949–1955) was a blueprint for government development expenditures for a seven-year period, and was imposed upon Iran by the international lending agencies. During the war, the country had accumulated substantial reserves of foreign exchange, but these were inadequate to finance the size of plans felt necessary by the government. The government therefore applied for a loan to the newly created International Bank for Reconstruction and Development, but was informed that the bank would consider only applications for individual projects whose soundness had been tested by technical studies. It then employed an American engineering firm[6] to work within the Ministry of Finance and to recommend projects for consideration.

The plan decided upon called for public sector investment expenditures amounting to 21 billion rials ($656 million) over the seven-year period 1949–1956. But it was never really implemented owing to two major factors: (1) lack of skilled administrators in the Plan Organization and (2) the oil crisis of 1951 which cut off the flow of foreign exchange that had been earmarked for the plan.[7]

The plan, it should be noted, was neither a comprehensive one for the allocation of the country's resources nor even a plan for all government investment. Rather it was a list of projects that had been investigated at the prefeasibility level and endorsed by the engineering firm with little consultation with the ministries and other official agencies.

Iran's First Plan unfortunately set a series of precedents. Through the Second, Third, and to a certain extent Fourth Plans, nearly all the project evaluation and a large part of the project initiation were done by foreign consultants in conjunction with Plan Organization counterparts in Tehran. There has been little or no participation or discussion of the merits and alternatives by private groups. In fact, until the late 1960s very little planning was undertaken either within the federal ministries and agencies or in the provinces. Some of the federal ministries and agencies have been apathetic and tardy in submitting projects. Others have been hostile, refusing to disclose the information required by the Plan Organization for project evaluation. In the provinces those few projects submitted for inclusion in the plans have been visionary, nebulous, or improperly appraised. As a result, it has often seemed to the public and to other agencies of government that the Plan Organization was operating within a vacuum.

The Second Plan

Serious disruptions had followed the nationalization of the oil industry, and because of this the First Plan was abandoned in favor of the Second Plan, which was to cover the period 1955–1962. The Second Plan marks the point at which planning in Iran became a reality.

The Second Plan, like the First, was not a comprehensive plan, nor did it have a unified approach. It did not mention the private sector, nor did it include the total activities of the public sector. Essentially, it consisted of an investment program covering that portion of public funds under the control of the Plan Organization. Oil revenues were arbitrarily divided between the Plan Organization and the Ministry of Finance, with the result that planning remained neither total nor coordinated, and policies and strategies that governments usually articulate as the basis for economic development were not incorporated.

The document itself was an essay in platitudes rather than a statement of clarity, defining the objectives, priorities, strategy, and measures of resource mobilization to take place. Moreover, it was arranged in a series of unconnected chapters, each representing a particular economic sector—agriculture, industry, and so on.

In practice, therefore, the Second Plan was simply a list of projects to be undertaken by the Plan Organization, and on which funds expected to be available from oil revenues were to be used.[8] Neither the planning document approved by the Parliament nor the reports supporting it were concerned with a systematic examination of the functioning of the Iranian economy; that is, the list of projects that made up the Second Plan did not fit into any systematically defined set of targets or goals for the economy. Indeed, there was no single theme or logical support to the selection of all the projects, and some implied objectives were incompatible with other implied objectives.

Because no specific statement of goals was identified, the criterion of success was essentially the extent to which the projects announced as part of the plan were completed.

Given the Second Plan's lack of attention to specific objectives, it is clear that it was impossible to give proper consideration to any conflicts between economic growth and other goals such as employment and income distribution.

The plan's expenditures were to be allocated to four major economic sectors: (1) agriculture-irrigation, (2) industry and mining, (3) transport and communications, and (4) social affairs. Expenditures were to be concentrated rather heavily in roads, dams, and other types of social overhead capital.[9] In retrospect, an examination of the Second Plan reveals a tendency of the planners to select projects with little potential for income generation and employment creation in the short run. Projects were few in number and highly capital-intensive. No attempt was made to compare the potential impacts that projects (for example, irrigation) within a sector would have. And no project rankings (based on rates of return) were undertaken.

In characterizing the final results of the plan, the only point that can be made is that project estimates were frequently low on the cost side and achievements were below forecast levels of attainment. The responsibility for this must be laid partly to administrative inefficiency, specifically in the area of cooperation between the Plan Organization and other government agencies, and to the lack of coordination between development policy and other economic policies, which should have been utilized by the government. In fact, it was this lack of coordination in such areas as expenditure levels and the creation of bottlenecks that induced inflationary pressures, a foreign exchange crisis, and a recession that plagued the economy from about 1960 to 1963.

Obviously, if the country's development process is viewed in terms of mathematical formulations of such idealistic patterns as balanced growth[10] or equilibrium growth, then the available evidence indicates that the plan was a failure. But to evaluate the country's performance in these terms (stable, sectoral expansion patterns or equilibrium growth) is to underestimate the complexity of the country's economic problems. The correct way of looking at Iran's development problems, one giving a broader perspective and one that sheds a different light on the Iranian situation, is to examine the economy as one suffering from a sociocultural constraint to growth rather than one constrained by financial resources.[11]

The size of the plan was well within Iran's ability to finance, but the organization and the managerial and labor inputs available to match the composition of projects to be included in the plan were inadequate; that is, in terms of skilled labor, managerial availability, and project preparation, Iran's ceiling was exceeded.

It was the scarcity of domestic resources that has caused a number of economists to argue that the plan was ''too big.'' Even in the economic sense, however, it is not completely clear that the oil revenues were being wasted by the plan. The reason is as follows: at that time, for Iran the most effective way to create the organization, managerial talent, and the skilled-labor supply essential to a successful sustained development effort was to provide its citizens with the opportunity to learn through directly participating in the development process. To argue that Iran should have postponed use of its foreign exchange earnings and borrowings until such time as its citizens had the necessary skills, and thus could utilize the funds at a later time when the rate of return on investment would be higher because of a more skilled-labor force, implies that the creation of the required talents could only be accomplished by some educational or on-the-job training program within the existing industrial sector. There is no evidence to indicate that such a process has been or would be effective in Iran.

This conclusion is borne out by measurements of growth during this period, which indicate that increases in national income originating in such sectors as manufacturing operated by older industrialists came from the input of resources, including capital equipment and labor, rather than through increased production per worker. Furthermore, the gains in average labor productivity in the manufacturing plants during the Second Plan period reflected mainly the installation of more capital equipment per worker, considerable work reorganization, and improved supervision, with little gain owing to improvement in worker efficiency. Increases in the labor productivity traceable to improved quality of the workforce were hindered by the persistence of traditional, irrational methods of worker selection, lack of or ineffectiveness of skill training programs, and inadequacy of social and financial workers' incentives.

The poor performance of the industrial workforce was most typical of the factories under the control of traditional management. The owner/managers of these factories were usually former bazaar merchants who had little concern for questions of productivity and efficiency and held traditional attitudes toward the value of labor (including a failure to acknowledge the existence of skill differences). Most of these employers discounted their real skill needs and recruited rural labor willing to work for low wages but with little capacity for industrial work, ignored the need for any genuine in-service skill training, and utilized their inadequately qualified workforces inefficiently and wastefully in largely unsupervised operations.[12]

The key to this line of argument rests in trying to evaluate Iran's present state of development and particularly its level of development at the time of the Second Plan in terms of a development sequence. The economy at the time of the Second Plan was still essentially a feudal society, and as a result was extremely rigid both in terms of socioeconomic mobility and in responding adequately to economic incentives. In fact, the social arrangements deeply ingrained in the society were the antithesis of those necessary to facilitate economic growth. The prime goal of the Second Plan, therefore, could not be a leap into a state of balanced and sustained equilibrium growth, but rather had to be a more limited one of uprooting and eventually replacing a mode of behavior that for centuries had been responsible for the almost complete absence of economic change. Perhaps the most effective development strategy under these conditions was, as in the Second Plan, a development program that exposed the economy to a number of alien technologies, ideas, and pressures. The initial result of the plan was cultural change through an institution-destroying phase. Once completed, the stage was set for the Shah's White Revolution. Development plans in Iran must therefore be evaluated not only in strict economic terms but also in terms of their ability to create an atmosphere that will permit the emergence of new workers with abilities and motives conducive to the establishment of a set of institutions and attitudes capable of creating the potential for endogenous growth.

Obviously from an economic standpoint, because it was divorced from economic analysis (for example, rates of return, cost-benefit analysis), the Second Plan must be considered a disaster. However, on noneconomic grounds, it may have represented the best strategy at the time; that is, it was able to identify correctly Iran's institutions to the extent to which those institutions were incompatible with high levels of sustained growth on a national or sectoral level. In effect the plan was able to modify those institutions in a direction so that at some point in the future the economy would be able to effectively utilize increases in resources such as oil revenues.

The Third Plan

The Third Plan, covering the period 1962 to 1968, was Iran's first effort at comprehensive planning. Its basic components[13] were an investment program for the public sector and some forecasts for the private sector, with primary emphasis on achieving a rate of growth of 6 percent per annum. Secondary objectives were (1) to enlarge employment possibilities, (2) to achieve a more equal distribution of income, and (3) to maintain relative price stability and equilibrium in the balance of payments.

Although it was explicitly stated in the plan that growth was to be combined with a greater attention to social justice, the treatment of these questions in any systematic manner was never attempted. For example, the goal of employment creation was ranked well below the goal of income growth, and the other goals mentioned were never tested or examined for possible tradeoffs.

The size of the plan was approximately 230 billion rials ($3.06 billion) for the public sector and 150 billion rials ($2.0 billion) for the private sector. No rationale was given for the selection of the figure for the private sector or how it would be offset by public sector expenditures.

Also, as in the Second Plan, the machinery of planning did not consider the joint effects on growth and social justice nor did it provide even a simple integration between public sector programs and private sector activities.

From a methodological point of view, therefore, the plan had a number of serious deficiencies. No formal economic models or programming methods were used, and no attempts were made to ascertain if there was a balance between the demand for and supply of such items as foreign exchange. Rather the basic method of planning resembled a "stage method" of planning, that is, a trial-and-error process.

As in the Second Plan, four broad sectors received the bulk of funds: (1) agriculture, (2) industry, (3) transport, and (4) social affairs. Because the planners lacked reliable data, however, they could not set specific quantifiable goals. Therefore, as in the case of national goals, all the sectoral allocations had to be determined on the basis of trial-and-error procedures. In practice this meant relying heavily on the subjective judgment of the planners.

Moreover, the administrative machinery[14] in the Plan Organization and the various ministries did not match the requirements for successful implementation of the plan; that is, the project identification and analysis that should have been undertaken by Plan Organization in consultation with the various ministries were never undertaken. Consequently, from the start the Third Plan was deficient in concrete projects for investment. The projects selected were chosen without sufficient analysis of their rates of return or their effect on other projects. The projects finally implemented under the plan tended to represent a shift in emphasis from social overhead capital to more productive activities, but it cannot be inferred that this change from the Second Plan was part of any well-conceived strategy.

The Third Plan has left a marked imprint on the country because it was characterized by a number of events that still affect the outlook of many government officials and what they expect of planning. First, the recession during which the plan was begun forced the government to speed up whatever development projects were forthcoming, irrespective of the priorities established in the plan.

Second, the Third Plan was just being completed when the Shah introduced his White Revolution. In particular, his far-reaching land reform exceeded by far the accomplishments that the planners, especially in the Ministry of Agriculture, would have dared to suggest in the plan or upon which they were basing their development strategy. These changes in direction and apparent lack of adaptability in planning strengthened the position of those government officials who believed that it was the right political decision at the right time that really counted in the success or failure of the development of the country. They further argued that formal development planning was too cumbersome and in any case impossible to implement. Their conclusion was that plans should be only an expression of intent, to be revised as often as necessary.

Third, these arguments were strengthened by a substantial increase in oil revenues over the original estimates, which necessitated major adjustments in the original plan. No mechanism for this eventuality had been provided for in the plan; as a result, the only adjustments that could be made were simply those of indiscriminate increases in allocations to public sector development. The original plan document, for all practical purposes, ceased being used as a reference during the plan period. The final outcome of the changes resulting from the higher revenues was a rate of economic growth exceeding 8 percent per annum, with important breakthroughs in the industrialization of the country and far-reaching changes in the social structure (arising from the reforms undertaken under the White Revolution).

Generally, the high rates of economic growth achieved during this period without resort to sophisticated economic analysis resulted in two basic attitudes emerging among a number of government officials. Some officials still doubt the necessity for or the capability of technicians and planners to predict events in a rapidly changing society and economy; they do not feel that the plans produced by the Plan Organization should be taken very seriously, especially when political intuition suggests a decision in a different direction from that recommended by the planners. Other officials, particularly a number of younger technocrats at the lower levels of government, feel that planning can make a significant contribution to accelerating development but only if medium-term plans are drawn up that establish specific longer-range targets. The general consensus among this group is that the responsibilities of each public body and of the private sector must be well defined, and a system must be established that requires periodic evaluation of the medium-term (five-year) plan at relatively short intervals so that the planners could determine the extent of deviation from the original targets and make recommendations appropriate for their revision. This procedure could then allow for plans to form the basis upon which short-term decisions could be made with respect to such matters as annual budget, import-export regulations, monetary policy, and fiscal policy.

This group further believes that a long-term 25-year horizon was necessary in the planning process, since a systematic approach to such issues as oil depletion could be made rationally only within this time frame.[15] From its planning experience through the first three plans, it became quite clear to this younger group of technocrats that objectives such as growth, income distribution, employment, balance-of-payments equilibrium, price level stability, and similar other objectives are interrelated—they are both competitive goals and mutually reinforcing. As a result, these planners began to feel that the country's traditional approach to planning—that is, short run or partial examination of one objective, often neglecting the interrelationships in the economy—though useful for some purposes, was nevertheless incomplete and quite often very misleading in terms of the policy prescriptions. Their conclusion was that planning in Iran should concentrate on the distinction between short-run and long-run effects of various actions. Tradeoffs among objectives and different policy instruments in both the short run and long run would have to be determined before a well-thought-out consistent, efficient, and feasible policy could be formulated.

The Fourth Plan

The Fourth Plan,[16] covering the period 1968–1972, began to incorporate some of the innovations to planning recommended by the technocrats, and in this sense it was an improvement over the previous plans in terms of both formulation and implementation. This was evidenced by a greater degree of comprehensiveness, as noted in the following overall objectives:

1. An increase in the rate of economic growth through gradually increasing the relative importance of industry, raising the productivity of capital, and using modern techniques of production
2. A more equitable distribution of income through employment and welfare policies
3. A decrease in the dependence on foreign countries in meeting basic requirements and a diversification of exports
4. An improvement in administrative services by the introduction of basic changes in the administrative system and the extension of advanced managerial techniques to all ministries and private organizations

Quantitatively, the Fourth Plan set an overall growth rate target of 9 percent per annum or an increase in GNP over the five-year period. It also set targets for employment whereby the number of jobs was projected to rise by 966,000 over the life of the plan. Iran's foreign exchange reserves were planned to increase by $600 million. However, when it came to setting targets for price stability and income distribution, no specific figures were given.

The total size of the Fourth Plan was originally put at 810 billion rials, with public sector expenditures set at 480 billion rials, or 59 percent of all investment outlays. During implementation, however, the public sector's share was raised several times until near the end of the plan period it reached 555 billion rials. As in previous plans, the means by which the private sector was to participate in the development effort were not specified. Also despite increased economic sophistication and comprehension of the subtleties involved in planning, the method of formulating the Fourth Plan was still based on trial and error. The plan was prepared in a number of stages undertaken entirely by the economists of the Plan Organization. The process started by estimating total investment requirements on the basis of the overall growth rate target, and sectoral investment allocations were fixed on the basis of sectoral production targets.

Five broad sectors were considered for planning: (1) agriculture, (2) industry, (3) oil and gas, (4) water and power, and (5) services. The main problems in drawing up the plan were, as in the past, lack of statistics, no basis for consistency, a shortage of concrete projects, and uncertainty concerning the availability of funds for the plan budget. The priorities, as inferred from its investment program, favored services, especially social overhead capital, which suggested a shift from directly productive activities that had been given a high priority in the Third Plan.

As with the Third Plan, most of the quantitative objectives were overachieved; that is, growth of GDP was approximately 10 percent. In most sectors, except construction and agriculture, the targets were also surpassed. By contrast, the crucial balance-of-payments target was seriously underachieved.

The Fifth Plan

Starting with the Fifth Plan,[17] the administrative structure within the government has undergone a fundamental change. The Plan Organization's official name is now the Plan and Budget Organization (PBO). In addition to the PBO, a number of government agencies (Figure 4–1) are now directly or indirectly concerned with the planning process. They are the Council of Ministers and Economic Council, PBO, Ministry of Economic Affairs and Finance, and the State Organization for Administration and Employment.

Council of Ministers and Economic Council

The highest policy-making body in the government sector is now the Council of Ministers, which consists of twenty ministers and five minis-

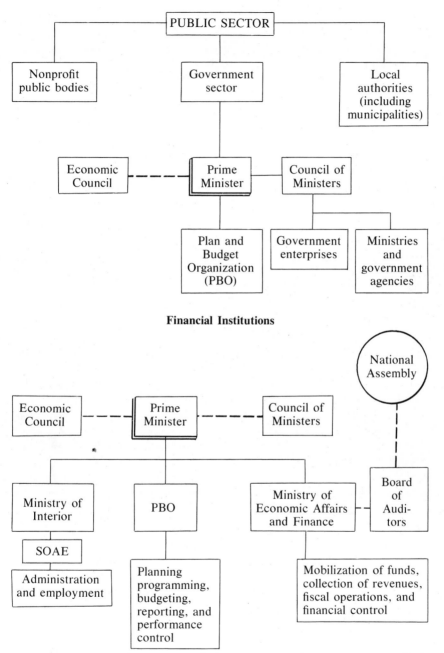

Financial Institutions

Source: Mehrad Ettehad, *An Approach to Government Budgeting in Iran* (New York: United Nations, 1974).

Fig. 4–1. Public Sector Structure.

ters of state; its chairman is the Prime Minister. The council makes final decisions regarding development planning, budgeting, and implementation.

Plan and Budget Organization

The basic functions of the PBO are:

1. To carry out social and economic surveys and studies so as to formulate plans and budgets and prepare social and economic reports
2. To prepare long-term plans in conjunction with executive agencies for submission to the Economic Council
3. To prepare quintennial development plans
4. To propose to the Economic Council guidelines and policies relative to the State General Budget
5. To exercise ongoing supervision over the country's statistical procedures and programs
6. To evaluate the productivity and performance of executive agencies and submit reports to the Prime Minister
7. To examine reports and questions that are to be discussed by the Economic Council
8. To determine the competence of and to classify consulting engineers and contractors
9. To establish standards, criteria, principles, and conditions of contracts relating to development projects
10. To determine and define terms of foreign loans and credits reserved for projects and programs
11. To control permanently the execution of all approved plans, programs, activities, and projects by the executive agencies
12. To keep the Prime Minister informed of the progress of programs, projects, and activities with respect to work programs proposed, work actually initiated, and work completed
13. To prepare and present biannual progress reports in conjunction with development projects and programs, and also compile and submit annual economic reports and comprehensive operating reports for each planning period
14. To contribute to the promotion of regional planning, budgeting, and administration to achieve a balanced interregional development through decentralization within the national context
15. To establish a national data system

Ministry of Economic Affairs and Finance

The Ministry of Economic Affairs and Finance is responsible, in cooperation with the PBO, for forecasting revenues and other resources needed for development expenditures and for mobilizing the funds required for the implementation of government programs. It is also responsible for the collection of government revenues. All government receipts and payments are consolidated in the treasury, which is an integral part of the ministry. In other words, all the fiscal operations of the government sector are managed by the ministry, which is also responsible for financial control both during and after the execution stage of the budget and for the preparation of the Budget Settlement Bill.

State Organization for Administration and
Employment (SOAE)

The functions of SOAE are:

1. To formulate and coordinate the activities for improving the management and organization of the government sector
2. To propose solutions to problems of government organizations
3. To conduct a program of management studies, research, and services designed to promote management methods and procedures
4. To guide and advise government agencies in improving management and organization

These reforms in administration have had the effect of consolidating power with the Economic Council. This council—not the PBO—selects the nation's development strategy and the projects to be included within the development plans. Its power derives from several conditions: (1) officials have continuous access to the Shah, which is a tremendous advantage in a country whose political system centers on one person; (2) because of its coordinating nature and formally limited functions, it can remain aloof from the mainstream of political and personal conflict that is daily in evidence in the ministries and other official government agencies; (3) it has become a depository and clearinghouse for vital economic information, only a part of which is available to other government agencies; (4) through informal contacts with all the entities participating in public sector investment, it is able to influence them without having to share in the responsibility for setbacks encountered in the actual execution of individual projects.

This change in administrative machinery was not a sudden break in the country's planning procedures, since the power of the Plan Organization had begun to erode in the early 1960s. In part, though, these administrative changes simply reflect the increasing competence of individual ministries to carry out their own research and project evaluation. The PBO is run essentially as a research organization whose task is to prepare documents and studies related to the overall economy and particularly to the sectors. From these studies the PBO makes recommendations to the individual ministries concerning project selection, financing, and so on. Since the PBO has no real power, however, the ministries frequently go their own way and implement projects given a low priority by the PBO.

Under the new organization, the PBO has had two choices in terms of its role and function in the planning process: (1) to meet directly any opposition from the ministries or other government officials, and (2) to accommodate itself to the existing situation both by sidestepping issues rather than meeting them head-on and by avoiding conflicts rather than resolving them. Because of their ambivalent position in the bureaucratic and political establishment, the planners in PBO are prone to choose accommodation. This has taken three forms: (1) to satisfy everybody, (2) to spread authorization for projects around to as many agencies and areas as possible, and (3) to postpone the evil day when oil revenues begin to decline and eventually cease altogether.

Satisfying everyone has been the simplest means of avoiding conflict. Because of the country's abundant revenues from oil, Iranian planners have not had to worry about priorities and thus have avoided tough choices. For example, since there has been little restraint on funds for industrial development, little emphasis has been placed on the preparation of a detailed sectoral plan for each sector, in which a formal choice had to be made between alternative projects on the basis of their comparative rates of return.

In trying to spread expenditures around, the philosophy of planners has been that if all cannot be satisfied, none need go entirely without. By assuming a massive expenditure during the Fifth Plan, for example, hard allocative choices have been avoided.

The plan's goals are written in unusually courageous farseeing language. These documents remain above controversy because they are wholly detached from current measures designed to achieve them. For example, the principal priorities of the revisions of the Fifth Plan have been a higher rate of economic growth, more equitable distribution of income, and assurance of national sovereignty in economic affairs. However, these goals may not be compatible with each other, and in any case it is doubtful whether they are capable of simultaneous implementation; to be significant, the plans must be given some kind of priority in terms of quantifiable levels of achievement. In short, the Iranian planning machinery is still deficient when it comes to implementation because there is simply no concrete set of goals on which to base the selection of projects.

The PBO's documents are still written in vague language, and it is impossible to discover how they are organized, in what way they are reorganized, in what manner they are made suitable, and by which means they are connected. The point stands out in relation to social progress; aims are recorded, but the plans are silent on specific policies. Apparently, future economic growth is expected automatically to take care of such matters as unemployment and social inequality.

Conclusions

The first conclusion to be drawn from the Iranian experience in the field of economic development planning is that, over the entire period of the country's modern (post-World War II) history, conscious efforts (although not too well organized) have been made by successive development plans to create conditions conducive to accelerated economic growth and to give priority to economic development over immediate gains in social welfare, even though the Fifth Plan seems to represent a swing toward expanded social welfare programs.

Second, despite numerous administrative problems still existing in the planning process, no one in official government circles questions the desirability of state activity and participation in the economy.

Third, since the early 1950s, Iran has made considerable progress toward the acceptance of another important idea: that a developing economy—especially one with rich oil reserves—needs overall programming and planning even if it has reached or is about to reach levels of per capita income corresponding to some of the Southern European nations.

Fourth, with passage of time together with the increasing complications of managing with reasonable efficiency a government apparatus comprising a rapidly growing and formidable array of public agencies, public opinion (including some leading representatives of private enterprise) has begun to give more and more weight to the arguments of the growing class of economic technocrats. In turn, the latter agree that because of past wastes involved in spending the nation's oil revenues, a more comprehensive approach to planning is needed.

According to the technocrats, successful economic planning in Iran involves coordinated action at three separate stages: (1) defining overall and accessible economic policy goals, (2) elaborating a national development plan, and (3) administering the plan and controlling the performance of the different sectors of the economy.

Fifth, with regard to the existing political system, Iran has a number of advantages in terms of achieving these goals. The centralized structure of the Iranian political system, the increasing concentration of power in the hands of the Shah and his political party, and the overwhelming role of the Prime Minister—all in addition to the experience built up in the field of promoting economic development—represent a tremendous advantage for any agency attempting to define the aims of economic policy in such a way as to avoid contradiction. The fact is, however, that no one in Iran has yet successfully arrived at such a definition.

The potential advantage of a strong central government, or more accurately of an extremely strong Prime Minister, is offset to a large extent by the diffusion of political and economic power within and without the government. The fact that for all practical purposes Iran's Prime Minister has no cabinet and that all the major issues are resolved directly between him, the Shah, and the minister or head of whatever ministry or department is immediately involved, with very little coordination with other interested government agencies, makes it exceedingly difficult to achieve unity of action among all potential policymakers, to say nothing of reaching general agreement on what the overall policy should be. This, of course, could be achieved if a strong Prime Minister had at his disposal a small group of policy advisers divorced from the daily political struggle and if he was willing to support them against pressures exerted from various sources. The fact that the Economic Council is a proper step in this direction does not alter the fact that it is still composed of ministers whose actions are under close scrutiny and none of which is considered by the Shah to be indispensable.

Sixth, and more important, even more serious obstacles to efficient planning emerge when we examine the problems involved in the management of the development plan and in control over the actions of the different sectors of the economy, as well as over the execution of regional development programs. In the light of past experience, it is unlikely that Iran can effect an orderly implementation of its development plans unless some basic and thorough reforms are made in public administration and in the legal and institutional structure of the public sector.

It may well be that in this respect Iran critically requires (1) establishing a civil service that embodies concepts of security and tenure, (2) eliminating the chronic problem of conflict of interest, and (3) lifting the veil of secrecy from the budgetary process. It is perhaps somewhat optimistically assumed here that the private sector would be willing to cooperate in executing a development plan if only for two reasons: (1) the stimulus given to the economy by a well-detailed national plan would increase investment and profit opportunities, and (2) the adoption of a definitive plan would force the authorities to substitute formal and impersonal rules for the present practice of solving issues and problems as they arise. The current practice is to resort to ad hoc administrative decisions which are as arbitrary as they are difficult to foresee.

These criticisms do not mean that coherent long-term planning of Iran's economic development cannot be achieved in the near future. It will be a rather difficult undertaking, however, because there are many diverse types of Iranians: the Iran of modern industrialists in the best tradition of nineteenth-century capitalism, the Iran of intellectuals of international renown and of illiterate village peasants, the Iran of honest political officials and professionals and of unscrupulous politicians. Were it otherwise, Iran would no longer be one of the world's many underdeveloped countries, and the problem of planning for development would probably not even arise. It has arisen, however, and with great urgency; and to entertain the belief that planning from high officials, without democratic participation by the country's population, represents the best possible solution is to fall prey to delusion.

Notes

1. Actually Reza Khan had begun planning in Iran through the initiation of a number of major national projects. Under his leadership planning was carried out on a rather ad hoc basis; for example, the famous railway from the Caspian Sea to the Persian Gulf was not based on any refined cost-benefit basis. Cf. P. Bjorn Oleson and P. Norregaard Rasmussen, "An Attempt at Planning in a Traditional State: Iran," in Everett E. Haten, ed., *Planning Economic Development* (Homewood, Ill.: Richard D. Irwin, Inc., 1963), pp. 223–24.

2. The process of consolidation of the Iranian national state is similar to that described for the European countries in the nineteenth century described by Assar Lindbeck, "The Changing Role of the National State," *Kyklos*, **28**: 23–45, 1975.

3. For a description of the unique features characterizing planning in oil-rich countries, see Jahangir Amuzegar, "Atypical Backwardness and Investment Criteria," *Economica Internazionale*, August 1960.

4. Ideology has, however, played some part in the manner in which Iran has approached economic planning. In contrast to Egypt, Syria, and Iraq, which are ideologically committed to "Arab socialism," and Lebanon and Saudi Arabia which are philosophically "capitalist," Iran has taken an intermediate position of "positive nationalism" or what is often referred to as "private enterprise assisted by the state." Cf. Jahangir Amuzegar, "Ideology and Economic Growth in the Middle East," *The Middle East Journal*, 1–2, 1975.

5. One often sees comparisons made between the approach taken to planning in Turkey and Iran. The presumption usually is made that both countries have a similar philosophical orientation toward planning. Neither the republican elitist regime in Turkey nor the monarchial reformist regime in Iran is, however, committed to any basic ideology or philosophical approach to planning. Economic incentives and social considerations both play a part in resource allocation and income distribution in the two countries. Both countries share with the private sector the chief responsibility for major developmental activities, reorganizing the role of private capital (domestic and foreign) in the process of capital formation and economic growth. The differences between the two countries' economic systems largely concern matters of national priorities and internal policies rather than basic philosophy of ideology. Cf. Amuzegar, *ibid.*, pp. 2–3.

6. Morrison-Knudsen International. The firm sent ten engineers and completed its work in four months. George Baldwin, *Planning and Development in Iran* (Baltimore: Johns Hopkins Press, 1967).

7. Jahangir Amuzegar, "Capital Formation and Development Finance," in Ehsan Yar-Shater, ed., *Iran Faces the Seventies* (New York: Praeger Publishers, 1971), pp. 67–68.

8. The Second Plan envisaged an initial expenditure of 70 billion rials in the public sector over the seven-year period. This was later increased to 84 billion rials, of which 75.2 billion rials was actually spent. Cf. *Report on the Operation of the Second Seven-Year Plan* (Tehran: Plan Organization, 1964), Appendix 5.

9. The plan covered only public investments under the control of the Plan Organization, the central development and planning body. The expenditures (see note 8 above) added up to only about one-half the total investments made in the public sector. The remainder was made by ministries and public agencies. Albert Waterson, *Development Planning: Lessons of Experience* (Baltimore: Johns Hopkins Press, 1965), p. 111.

10. The concepts of balanced growth and equilibrium growth have been analyzed extensively in the literature. An excellent summary is given in Janos Kornai, *Anti-Equilibrium* (Amsterdam: North Holland Publishing Co., 1971).

11. For a similar observation in a different context, see Albert Hirschman, "Obstacles to Development: A Classification and a Quasi Vanishing Act," *Economic Development and Cultural Change* 385–89, July 1965.

12. Cf. William Bartsch, "The Industrial Labor Force of Iran: Problems of Recruitment, Training and Productivity," *The Middle East Journal* 28–29, Winter 1971.

13. Division of Economic Affairs, *The Third Plan Frame,* 1341–1346 (Tehran: Plan Organization, 1961).

14. An excellent description of the planning process under the Third Plan is given in Baldwin, *Planning and Development in Iran*, chapters 3 and 8.

15. A start in this direction is Planometrics Bureau, *A Twenty Year Macro-Economic Perspective for Iran, 1351–1371* (Tehran: Planning Division, Plan and Budget Organization, May 1974), mimeo.

16. *Fourth National Development Plan, 1968–1972* (Tehran: Plan Organization, 1968).

17. *Iran's Fifth Development Plan, 1973–1978, Revised Summary* (Tehran: Plan and Budget Organization, May 1975).

5

Quantitative Approaches to Planning in Iran

Introduction

Once the goals of each plan are selected, the planning problem in Iran becomes one of outlining operational methods for mobilizing and allocating resources to reach those goals in the most efficient manner. Because there is usually a significant lag in the collection and processing of data concerning the progress achieved in key areas of the economy, the planners must be able to devise means of processing this information as inputs into the next plan. Their approach to quantifying the major economic forces at work in the economy must, therefore, be simplified by formulating them in somewhat abstract terms. It is the level of abstraction and the technical means used in achieveing that abstraction that surround the current debate over the merits of the type of planning now taking place in Iran.

Model Building in the Iranian Planning Process

Over time, mathematical models of the Iranian economy have been constructed at various levels of complexity, ranging from one or two equations involving the more important macroeconomic aggregates, such as the levels of investment needed to achieve a certain target rate of growth,[1] to complete systems of up to 200 equations involving the entire economy in great detail. Two path-breaking developments in economics have stimulated the whole spectrum of this planning methodology. The first of these was the Keynesian[2] formulation of macroeconomic models based on aggregates of the whole economy that can be statistically observed and used as the basis of the national income accounts of the country. The second development was made possible by the formulation by Leontief[3] of a multisector general equilibrium model of the simple linear type that enabled a consistent elaboration of a whole range of interdependent economic activities simultaneously. The two approaches nearly dovetail in the Iranian context, so that it was possible to begin with a very simple Keynesian macroeconomic model in the Third Plan and extend it into a more elaborate form in the Fourth Plan; and as computer capability and capacity has increased in the Plan Organization, it has been possible to increase the detail and sophistication of these models by first developing input-output techniques in the latter phases of the Fourth Plan and finally adopting linear programming in the Fifth Plan.[4]

As the Fifth Plan continues to be revised, these techniques consist of projections and estimates of the country's feasible level of output as determined through an identification of the likely constraints to growth, alternative compositions of that output based on certain assumptions regarding the country's future growth possibilities, and the authorities' priorities concerning a number of socioeconomic goals. Macroeconomic models are now used as a matter of course in the context of the country's planning and budgeting project evaluation exercises.

The use of mathematical models as a prime means of formulating the basic framework within which planning decisions are to be made has been resisted by many government officials, and even by some of the leading Iranian economists both within and outside the PBO. In general, the major skeptics in Iran of quantitative models of national economies, and in particular those developed to depict the Iranian economy, usually argue that less rigorous and more pragmatic approaches are more realistic and thus more effective in achieving the nation's major socioeconomic objectives.

In spite of widespread resistance to their application, however, macroeconomic models continue to be perfected both in the PBO and in the more progressive ministries. In this process their time horizon has been expanded from the earlier five-year forecasts to those capable of projecting rather accurately (given the stability of their assumptions) the country's major economic aggregates over a 25-year time horizon. The question naturally arises as to whether such models should be used directly as the basis of major policy decisions and whether they can easily supplement the more pedestrian methods (such as informed judgment of "experts") as guides to official planning work.

Development Characteristics, Economic Problems, and Model Choice

Ultimately the decision to use (and if so, in what manner) the alternative planning methodologies available to Iranian officials must depend on the relative ability of each planning method to depict accurately the major characteristics of the economy, particularly those that will have a major bearing on the country's potential for continued growth. In this connection five characteristics of the economy that must be amenable to quantification or at least to systematic qualification stand out in importance.

(1) The first and most important in terms of the problems it presents

to planners is that the economic system has developed to the point where it is constituted of a very complicated network of interrelationships. These interrelationships are increasing in number as the country becomes more industrialized and integrated, both internally and with the world market. In contrast to the situation existing twenty years ago, regions are not now engaged exclusively in subsistence activity; increasingly large numbers of people are producing either for the market or for themselves. This trend away from regional autonomy and toward specialization based on trade between regions, as well as assimilation of rural groups into the market economy, must be explicitly accounted for in the planning models.

(2) The second is that the economy's rapid growth rate has resulted in changes in the time lag between the point at which a policy action is undertaken by the government and the time that elapses before the brunt of its impact is felt. The cause of this phenomenon is undoubtedly a number of changing and new socioeconomic interrelationships. Since an avowed purpose of planning in Iran is to change a number of these interrelationships in order to accelerate growth, the approach to planning should therefore be dynamic in the sense of explicitly incorporating time patterns into a general analytical framework.

(3) The third is that the economy's productive structure lacks certain, perhaps many, important lines of production; that is, many of the cells of the national input-output tables are empty. A number of products are not produced at all but are supplied entirely by imports. A model of the economy, if it is to be useful in terms of identifying areas of investment, must be capable of separating these imports into those in which the country will (within a certain time) be competitive and those in which it will not.

(4) The fourth is that despite fairly high levels of tariffs and other restraints on trade, Iran is still a fairly open country. The degree of the nation's integration into the world economy has fluctuated over time, and there has been an attempt to achieve self-sufficiency in certain areas. It is clear, however, that outside influences are still unavoidable. As a consequence, and even though the country is currently taking great advantage of favorable trends in the world economy, there is no assurance that conditions will not become less favorable, so that trade may, in the near future, be a stifling limitation on the nation's desired pattern of development. Models used in forecasting must therefore be capable not only of identifying possible adverse trends in world markets but also of estimating the impact of these changes on the domestic economy.

(5) The fifth characteristic—and one related to the other four—is that planners are human and cannot foretell the future. It is obviously the purpose of planning to anticipate the future and if possible to shape it in

directions in line with the nation's objectives. Therefore it is necessary that the approach and methods used in development planning be suitable to indicate likely trends in economic activity over at least a 25-year time horizon.

All are essential to the formulation of a development plan that can be implemented in a manner that will significantly improve the performance of the economy. Yet they have caused a considerable amount of controversy in government circles in Iran. The major discussion centers on the degree of uncertainty inherent in making accurate forecasts of the major economic variables. Some older and more institutionally oriented administrator-economists in the government make forecasts by the "rule of thumb" or "commonsense" type, in contrast to the more sophisticated method of the younger technocrats using advanced econometric techniques. The older administrators argue that the advantage of the rule-of-thumb approach is mainly one of cost—econometric models are time-consuming and often very expensive to develop. The technocrats, however, are less impressed with the past performance of the rule-of-thumb approach, and they argue that this approach is not capable of bringing out the underlying assumptions (particularly quantitative) on which the planner's ultimate decisions must be based. The technocrats particularly stress the fact that in a rapidly changing environment, the rule-of-thumb approach is rather inflexible (since no real framework has been formulated within which alternatives can be executed and their implications analyzed), often leading to blind groping, in marked contrast to the systematic approach of the more mathematical planning tools; that is, mathematical models of the economy have the potential, with the development of computer technology, of being able to simulate the economy under a wide variety of situations and in a very rapid period of time.

Perhaps because of the recent upgrading of the quality of the mathematical models developed in Iran, the technocrats now have more influence with the decisionmakers at the PBO. But this has led to some difficulties since the model builders are often foreign technicians with no real knowledge of the Iranian society, its history, traditions, and in several notable cases even of its economic mechanisms. In contrast, the more institutionally (nonmathematically) inclined planners in the PBO are older Iranians with deep insight (albeit not quantifiable) into the workings of the country's development process. To synthesize these two schools of thought (or, more correctly, opposing views), we have developed the Hegelian model in the latter chapters of this book. This synthesis will help to provide insights into the long-run potential of the economy, insights which are impossible to achieve through exclusive use of either the institutional or the analytical approaches to planning.

The Use of Quantitative Techniques in Iranian
Development Planning

Quantitative methods include a number of mathematical techniques, such as that of statistical investigation applied in economic analysis, econometric methods, input-output techniques, and linear programming. Linear programming in particular is becoming especially popular in macroeconomic planning.[a]

In discussing these techniques as used in Iran, reference is made here to the activity being planned rather than to all the details and intricate technicalities of the methods themselves. In this manner, the techniques serve as the means of understanding problems, rather than as ends in themselves. This point is important because in planning, the problem should largely dictate the techniques that will be used. Unfortunately, in Iran this has not always been the case. The official plan documents in Iran are notoriously sketchy. For example, the early chapters of the documents usually give some general statement of the basic goals that the planners wish accomplished during the plan period. The goals are in turn quantified, and final levels of output are listed as the plan targets. No methodology on how the final targets are established is presented, which gives the impression that the planners have placed major reliance upon operationally meaningless projections of the economy. This is a fair criticism, for the connections between the general plan framework set forth in the earlier chapters of the document and the more specific industry and sector chapters that follow are tenuous; a number of the latter have the look of piecemeal agency programs.

Worst of all problems is the time phasing. No phasing of individual projects is specified but, instead all are presented in one single five-year lump.[b] For example, in the public sector very little provision is made for those projects that would need to be started in the latter part of one plan and completed early in the next if a steady thrust of expansion from plan to plan were to be maintained. Moreover, as plans have unfolded, many temporary industry inconsistencies have developed. For example, in the Fourth Plan, aluminum capacity was installed considerably ahead of the

---

[a] The Planometrics Bureau headed by Firouz Vakil was set up to extend this work and to develop models more applicable to the Iranian context.

[b] Most plans, at least the published versions, list only a few specific projects, with only a list of sectoral targets. Individual projects are then identified for implementation as the plan proceeds. At the beginning of the plan period, therefore, the authorities have only a vague idea of what activities will be undertaken in the various sectors, let alone any notion as to the optimal sequence of implementing these activities to attain the maximum contribution to the plan's goals.

requirement for it. Brick capacity lagged badly, and that of cement was even worse. Some of these difficulties were the result of physical problems that could not have been foreseen, but much of the trouble was chargeable to bad detailed planning.[5]

Planning Techniques in the Second Plan

The Second Plan (1955–1962), like its predecessor, was a series of government projects, with no macroeconomic framework for it. The sectoral investment allocation in the public sector was determined more by the availability of projects than by explicit long-term policy considerations. Most planners admit that few, if any, cost-benefit analyses on specific projects were performed, and those that were performed were undertaken independently of other projects; nor were estimations made of the contribution of these projects to the main goals of the plan.

This approach had a number of serious drawbacks. (1) Despite the active role played by the Plan Organization, a number of ministries and agencies still had control over the choice of projects in their sectors, and the criteria used for their decision were difficult to discern. (2) The need for simultaneous decisions in different sectors of the economy was obscured because of the independent priority setting of the ministries. (3) There was a tendency to ignore indirect effects, for example, expansion of the cotton textile sector which in turn requires expansion of other industries. (4) The concentration on project analysis made it impossible to monitor and control the overall level of expenditures.

The outcome of this process was fairly predictable. Within two years of the start of the plan, the Plan Organization discovered that the actual expenditures on projects had exceeded planned expenditures in two of the four main planning sectors, while a shortage existed in the other two. In the agriculture and irrigation sector, for example, substantial overspending occurred on large dam projects at the expense of crop investment, animal husbandry, and loans to farmers for small-scale irrigation projects. In the communications and telecommunications sector, heavy overspending on railways and roads was achieved at the expense of other facilities. Similarly, a small number of large textile factories absorbed a large amount of funds that could have provided for a wide range of industries. Because of the government's concentration in these areas, there was, owing to lack of funds, little expenditure on public health and rural development activities. Thus, in general, almost all the large-scale long-gestation projects were costing more than was expected—a situation which was also found during the Third and Fourth Plans.

As the foreign exchange reserves dwindled to zero, the International

Monetary Fund, supported by the World Bank, imposed a strict policy of restraint on the government's expenditures. The result of these cutbacks was almost three years of complete stagnation. It took a new plan and a large bonus payment in foreign exchange from a new oil concessionaire to bring the economy back to life.

Planning Techniques in the Third Plan

The Third Plan (originally for 5 years but extended to 5½, from mid-1962 to the end of 1967) was more comprehensive than were the previous two, in the sense that all major targets for the economy were stated in the plan. Still there was no indication in the plan document of the methods to be used to establish overall income targets. No macroeconomic framework existed for the analysis. It can be inferred, however, that the technique of commodity balances was used in an attempt to achieve consistency among sectoral output goals. Thus demand for private consumption was estimated on the basis of consumption expenditure elasticities and the expected growth rate of income, and exports and government expenditure were projected independently. The planners made an estimate of demand in the terminal year of the plan, and then determined the growth rate of output needed to balance the supply and demand.

The Third Plan also marked the first time that the Plan Organization had attempted systematically to take into consideration the impact of activities of the private sector on the growth of the economy. The planners believed that if estimates of the amount of private investment were made, the plan would be comprehensive. Unlike the First and Second Plans, which were composed of separate investment projects, the Third Plan was framed in global terms; that is, it attempted to include all investments in the various sectors of the economy so that their aggregate impact on the economy could be determined and thus estimates of an overall rate of growth for the economy could be established.

Once the Third Plan was under way, however, it was soon apparent that the analytical framework used—commodity balances plus the very simple assumption that changes in real income were simply a function of the capital stock—was not a reliable basis upon which to estimate the expenditures required for the target rate of growth. The ratio between investment and output is rarely stable, particularly in a country such as Iran, which was undergoing a major social (the White Revolution) and investment program. Thus as the development projects for each sector were prepared and approved, the planners were not able to determine the relationship between investment in the project, the project's contribution to its sector's goals, and the overall goal of the Third Plan.

Planning Techniques in the Fourth Plan

The Fourth Plan, scheduled from March 1968 to March 1973, was more sophisticated than previous plans in its analytical approach to the country's development. The planners set a target growth rate of 9 percent and set sectoral targets consistent with this rate. Representatives from the Plan Organization met regularly with the various ministries to take into account sectoral interrelationships and overall limitations and objectives, and they brought a great deal of practical experience to bear on the problems of expanding capacity and output in each sector and of integrating the sectoral plans.

Economists at the Plan Organization actively used the formal techniques of input-output analysis in preparing the plan. They estimated final demand for commodities by standard input-output methods and projected the necessary output to meet that level of final demand. Like the Third Plan, the investment requirements for the plan period were calculated from the sectoral targets by means of capital/output coefficients.[6]

Critical to the Fourth Plan and to growth analysis made in its preparation was the analysis of the interrelationship between economic sectors. As the target rate of growth was increased from 7 percent in the Third Plan to 9 percent in the Fourth Plan, it became clear that this rate of expansion could not be achieved if certain industries were unable to expand adequately. The sluggish output response anticipated in such sectors as agriculture created bottlenecks in the supply of goods to other industries that purchased their products. The result of such bottlenecks would be either a slowing down in the rate of growth or inflationary price raises. Thus the planners felt that an estimate of the necessary rates of output of all sectors could help greatly toward eliminating the shortages of essential inputs and allowing the higher rate of growth to develop without inflation.

In the Fourth Plan the technique of input-output analysis (interindustry projection) allowed planners to obtain a better estimate of the likely rates of growth in each of the major sectors—agriculture, manufacturing, and so on—that had not been possible previously.

This simple analytical tool allowed planners in the Plan Organization to anticipate those bottlenecks that would likely be present once the overall national target rate was set. And it was possible to forecast from the input-output chart precisely how much each industry and each sector needed to buy from and sell to every other industry in order to avoid shortages.

Planners in Iran continue to use input-output projections for several purposes. For example, the tables are often used to estimate labor requirements, by industry, and these are compared with labor supply in various geographic regions. This allows the planners to determine, among other things, the amount of new housing required in the region to service the expanding workforce. Also, the planners have used input-output tables to look for sectors in which specific projects are most likely to have a high rate of return, that is, for industries that are expected to produce products in great demand, given the overall goals and sectoral targets of the plan.

Despite their usefulness and expanded application in planning decisions, input-output techniques have become one of the most controversial elements in the Iranian planning process, and attacks on their use have been numerous. Three principal faults are cited by the critics.[7] The first and most damaging is the problem of aggregation and the validity of a production function by industry. The metal products industry, the agricultural industry, the mining industry, and so on are not homogeneous groups of entities in Iran, but are heterogeneous, as a result of the dualism existing in the country, that is, the presence and coexistence of large modern firms in the same industry as smaller traditional firms. But obviously, not all firms within each industry produce the same type of product and at the same costs. For example, an increase in the agricultural industry will create demands for inputs depending on which individual crops are expanded. Some of the criticism of the use of input-output techniques for planning would thus be removed if, instead of grouping together all firms in a sector, the tables were constructed by breaking down each industry into a modern and traditional set of firms, each presumably with their own distinct output and input requirements.

The second criticism of input-output techniques is that they assume linearity; that is, they assume that if inputs into a sector double, output will also double. This assumption overlooks the fact that many plants in Iran are operated at less than full capacity: as output increases within these plants, the proportion of fixed cost to total declines; if a larger plant is substituted, fixed costs probably increase. It is not proper, therefore, to project a new input-output table for Iran by simply multiplying the function of the old by a given coefficient of expected production increase.[8]

The final criticism of the use of these techniques in Iranian planning is that they are unable to handle technological innovation. New techniques are being rapidly introduced from abroad and continue to change the proportion and type of inputs used to produce a given level of output. Not only that, but new goods and services will be produced each year; new industries not previously known will be called forth. Since very little of the interindustry structural relationships existing at the start of the plan will be present at the completion of the plan period, the critics argue that the quantitative goals set for the plan in its draft stages are totally without foundation.

Supporters of input-output employ three main counterarguments. First they argue that in day-to-day planning and revisions, the input-output tables are being continually revised and adjusted by engineering estimates that are capable of taking into account the individuality of new products and technologies within a sector. Second, they argue that the tables are not the only analytical tools used, but instead are only one of a number of tools used in analyzing the economy. In fact their current role is simply that of a crude instrument whose basic function is to draw attention to economic gaps that might not otherwise be noticed.

Technical considerations aside, a serious problem inherent in the input-output approach is that there is no objective rationale for choosing sectors to be emphasized in the plan.[9] Also the system is potentially capable of achieving consistency[10] only after sectoral final demand targets have been determined. In the case of Iran, final demand will be determined simply by the Shah or the Economic Council without considering the interaction between production and consumption. The result is often to set a series of goals that, given the interrelationships in the economy, are not consistent. Very few planners have had the courage to tell the Shah that his goals are not feasible because they are inconsistent in terms of the country's resources. The inability of the plans to achieve their goals is then construed by the Shah and other government officials as a sign of incompetence on the part of the planners.[11]

Planning Techniques in the Fifth Plan

The models used prior to the Fifth Plan for work related to planning and forecasting were consistent models (balancing of supply and demand) rather than planning models involving optimization. In the Fifth Plan, optimizing models were used as exploratory tools in the initial stages of the preparation of the plan, but they were never incorporated into the official document or even widely circulated. Thus it is useful to examine some of the problems that these types of models entailed in the Iranian planning context, their implications for policy making in Iran, and how far they contribute to answering some of the major problems of choice involved in the country's future planning exercises.

One of the models developed for the Fifth Plan was the Battelle linear programming model.[12] The model was constructed to examine different aspects of the economy resulting from changes in government policy. Because of the increasing concern in Iran over unemployment, the model was designed specifically to determine what policies would have to be undertaken to prevent unemployment from rising above 8,850,000 workers; the government did not want unemployment to be above 3 percent of the labor force in 1977.

The linear programming results (Table 5–1) indicated how this target could be met while at the same time achieving the government's major objective—the maximization of personal consumption during the plan period (1973–1977).[13]

In terms of their ability to increase the level of personal consumption, food and tobacco processing were most efficient. In addition, the model recommended that emphasis should also be placed on expanding the construction and social services sectors. In contrast, sectors that were unlikely to contribute significantly to the plan's objectives were (1) manufacturing, (2) metals and metal products, and (3) textiles and carpets. Given the level of production (Table 5–1), the model then estimated the contribution that labor would make to increasing personal consumption if workers were allowed to move from one sector to another. Thus, for example, in the case of services and construction, total personal consumption would rise by 326,000 rials over the plan period (1973–1977) if an additional worker would be allowed to move into this sector, provided that all other constraint levels specified in the model were held constant.

To make a linear programming model of the Battelle type realistic and meaningful in Iran, so that it may be used by the planners as a basis for decision making, several conditions are required: (1) the data must be of

Table 5–1

Total Output by Sector Determined by the Linear Programming Model for Iran—1977 (billion rials 1972 prices)

Sectors	1969	1977	Average Annual Rate of Growth, 1967–1977
Livestock	82	114	4.2
Crops	120	208	7.1
Forestry and Fishing	5	29	35.0
Mining	9	47	23.0
Oil and Gas	284	525	8.0
Construction	132	276	9.6
Food and Tobacco	113	267	11.4
Metals and Metal Products	73	85	1.9
Chemicals and Petrochemicals	97	205	9.8
Nonmetallic minerals	23	49	9.9
Textiles and carpets	91	98	1.0
Other manufacturing	48	29	−6.2
Transportation	61	129	9.9
Public Utilities	53	105	8.9
Trade and Commerce	255	399	5.8
Social Services	55	145	12.8
Total	1501	2708	7.5

Source: M. Borlin and R. Looney, *Battelle Linear Programming Model of Iran* (Tehran: The Plan Organization, 1972), p. 50.

sufficient quality to depict accurately the forces actually at work in the economy, (2) it must be possible to make accurate forecasts needed by the model, and (3) the model must be adaptable to the socioeconomic or institutional environment in which planning takes place.

The quality of data gathered for the model was probably not adequate at the time that work began on the Fifth Plan (1972) for linear programming. In the case of the Battelle model, the technical coefficients used in formulating the input-output tables were obtained not as is usually done by an analysis of historical data but through interviews. From a statistical sample of firms and establishments in each of the sixteen sectors used in the model, a set of questions concerning inputs, sales, and so on were asked of the plant owner or manager. Given the fact that few companies kept records, or certainly records of this type, it was not surprising that there was a tremendous variation in responses—even from firms which on the surface looked as though they were quite similar in terms of the products they produced.

It was also impossible to check the validity of the input-output coefficients with other estimates since the sectors selected for the Battelle table did not coincide with those used for the Ministry of Economy's 1965 input-output table (the only other input-output table of the economy). Hence, it was impossible to make a comparison of any possible trends in the country's productive patterns. Instead, the interviewers produced what was referred to as an *ex ante* input-output table for 1977. In doing so, the firms interviewed were asked to estimate their likely change in techniques of production, technology, and factor inputs over the five-year plan period.

This produced a greater variation in answers obtained when firms were asked what their existing input-output relationships were. Obviously, data of this quality were not capable of yielding equal results on inputs into the country's planning process.

Given reasonable data, the great value of linear programming is that the objective function, once selected, can be achieved to the maximum extent, given the country's available resources. The point is to minimize political pressures for "pet projects" or "empire builders" by the ministries. In the case of Iran, however, the model and its objective function (to maximize personal consumption) were very much conditioned by the organizational structure of the government. For linear programming to become effective, the politicians must be willing to accept the results once the objective is set. In the Battelle model, the objective function initially given (presumably by the Shah and approved by the Economic Council) was to maximize personal consumption. The results of the model indicated that to meet that objective, the agricultural sector should not be given a high priority in the plan; that is, other sectors were more efficient in terms of achieving this goal. The Ministry of Agriculture, however, induced the Economic Council to reject the model's results. Several other objective and constraints functions were then injected into the model to ascertain if agriculture could make a greater contribution to such goals as GNP growth. It did not. In any case the model was rejected probably not because of its poor data base but because once the results determined in an objective function were presented, it became apparent to a number of government officials that their ministries would not receive their usual allocations and that the system of decision making in Iran, based mainly on family power, personal favors, family connections, and loyalties, would be replaced by harsh economic realities. The agricultural sector then received the highest priority in the development strategy adopted for the Fifth Plan.

With the rejection of linear programming as a basis for comprehensive decision making, the Fifth Plan was assembled on an ad hoc basis. And the planners reverted to selecting projects on an individual basis, often without even the most rudimentary cost-benefit analysis being performed. As a result, sectoral targets were obtained on the basis of imprecise methods: guesses, intuition, and so on.

The weaknesses of the Fifth Plan were:

1. The relationship between macrotargets and sectoral targets was never clearly spelled out.
2. Social indicators were not identified in any meaningful sense for the purpose of integrated sectoral planning.
3. Regional planning was not integrated into the plan. Instead a budget was set aside for projects that were assumed to be of a strictly regional nature and solely for the purpose of improving that (presumably lower-income) region's standing.

In revising the Fifth Plan, certain significant improvements have been made so that relatively consistent if not optimal development targets can be achieved. The revised plan now includes the following:

1. It estimates the total financial resources over the plan period, categorizing resources by rials and foreign exchange income and breaking them down according to private and public sectors.
2. It proposes alternative investment packages on the basis of the public sector's resources. These packages include private sector estimates as well as growth rate implications for the various sectors.
3. It identifies bottlenecks and immediately focuses attention on plans to relieve those constraints. Priorities are adjusted accordingly.
4. It derives a macroframework, in keeping with employment, mone-

tary, fiscal, and balance-of-payments objectives, and details potentially achievable overall growth rates in consumption, investment, and government spending.

5. It also provides that sectoral planning committees draw up the growth requirements of each sector, their constraints, and the targets toward which they should be aiming.

6. With the totality of the plan funds more or less agreed upon, the allocation process at the sector level begins, bearing in mind the overall and sectoral objectives. It is at this level that income distribution is considered on an ad hoc basis in the emphasis to be given to the social sectors vis-à-vis the production and infrastructures sectors.

Obviously the process of organizing a comprehensive and consistent plan is iterative. But it is never clear when the process of iteration is to stop and the final figure agreed upon.

The most difficult part of the plan is to gear the sectoral allocations toward plan objectives and to ensure the consistency of various sectoral targets. It is usually the case that the initial sectoral requirements by far exceed the initial macrobudget, and the consistency requires in the first place harmonizing aggregates. Again this is done on an iterative ad hoc basis with no assurance that any degree of consistency with the macrolevel objectives has been achieved.

Conclusions

A number of mathematical models of varying complexity have been developed in Iran as aids in the planning process. At present, the more elaborate models such as linear programming can be used only at a research level. It appears, however, that they will eventually have the potential to contribute to the overall upgrading of the efficiency of the country's development efforts.

Iran's planning experience, using a wide variety of economic models, has brought out some pertinent points regarding the limitations of these tools. First, at the present time macromodels combined with an input-output framework give reliable results for only relatively short time periods.

Second, in planning at the ministerial level, partial models such as that for agriculture are currently in a position to go into greater detail using the input-output and linear programming techniques. With their experience at data gathering and an awareness of changes in technology, the individual ministries are now able to update the critical parameters of these models.

Third, it appears that the existing approach to project selection in Iran now used in the Fifth Plan, while lacking in sophistication, is adequate though in need of refinement to eliminate some existing inconsistencies. The planning process, as set up now, appears capable of identifying white elephants and preventing their selection; at the same time the level of ministerial competence has increased to the point where a large number of solid, if not of maximum potential, projects can be identified.

Nevertheless one major weakness still exists—the absence of any long-term framework into which each of the successive (five-year) plans can be integrated. Continuity of this type is essential if the national objective of achieving by the end of the century a dynamic, self-sufficient (from oil revenues) economy capable of creating high levels of employment and a more equitable distribution of income is to be reached.

Notes

1. For an excellent description of the development of mathematical tools as aids in the Iranian planning process, see Yousef Badii, "A Development Program for Iran," unpublished Ph.D. dissertation, University of Cincinnati, 1973.

2. As developed along the lines by Laurance Klein. See Laurance Klein and Jere Behrman, "Econometric Growth Models for the Developing Economy," L. Klein, ed., *Essays in Honour of Sir Roy Harrod* (London: Oxford University Press, 1971), pp. 167–87. Klein and Behrman note that special attention should be made to the special characteristics of developing countries if Keynesian models (which were designed for the more advanced countries) are to be applied to the less developed nations. These include: (1) trade, with special emphasis on exports of primary commodities and the composition of imports between capital goods, consumer goods, and fuel; (2) sector composition of production and supply (primary, secondary, tertiary); (3) income distribution; (4) prices and inflation; and (5) politicoeconomic institutions. They note that these considerations are looked upon as refinements in model building for the industrial countries, but they are of primary importance for the developing economy. It is clear, however, that both income distribution and politicoeconomic institutions have been deficient in the models constructed for planning purposes in Iran.

3. Dr. A. S. Schaheen of the Ministry of Economy has pioneered developing the Leontief input-output tables. See his 1965 input-output table for Iran reproduced in Appendix B of this book.

4. A number of linear programming plans developed simultaneously

for use in drawing up the Fifth Plan. Unfortunately, little coordination existed between the teams working on these models. The one developed by the Battelle team led by Max Borlin is discussed in this chapter. The Plan Organization had its own model, as did at least one other agency. The Ministry of Agriculture's table produced by a team from M.I.T. was developed by the International Labor Organization. Cf. Graham Pyatt et al., *Employment and Income Policies for Iran, Mission Working Paper No. 12, Methodology for Macroeconomic Projections* (Geneva: International Labor Organization, 1973), mimeo. Instead of duplicating efforts (each had its own data collecting team), more useful tables could have been obtained from one major collaboration.

5. For a detailed breakdown of the expenditures and allocations under the early plans, see Ahmed Saboonchi Isphani, "The Optimization of Economic Resources for Economic Growth in Iran," unpublished Ph.D. dissertation, University of Southern California, 1966.

6. "Econometric Models for the Fourth Plan," *Tahqiqat-e Eqtesadi*, **5**:48–61 for a description.

7. The limitations of analytical techniques such as input-output analysis have been discussed at length in the literature; our comments here apply only to those discussed in Iran. For a summary of the objections to applying these techniques in developing countries, see John Pawelson, *Latin America: Today's Economic and Social Revolution* (New York: McGraw-Hill, 1964), chapter 10.

8. This is the fundamental explanation of the empirical relationship between productivity growth and output growth, a relationship first observed by Verdoon and now referred to in the literature as Verdoon's law. Cf. Nicholas Kaldon, *Strategic Factors in Economic Development* (Ithaca, N.Y.: Cornell University Press, 1967), chapter 1, for a detailed explanation of these phenomena.

9. Of course linear programming overcomes this deficiency by specifying an objective function, such as personal consumption, which is to be maximized over the time period. The ability of the various sectors to contribute to this objective in turn determines their proper level of output and expansion during the plan framework. Cf. Max Borlin and Robert Looney, *The Battelle Linear Programming Model for Iran* (Tehran: Plan Organization, 1972), mimeo.

10. There are four main consistency tests: (1) Overall balance of final resources and expenditures—the proposed volume of total expenditures must be matched by an equal volume of resources to finance it. For example, there must be a balance between foreign exchange resources and expenditures. (2) Consistency of sectoral and overall objectives—the sectoral programs in aggregate serve the general objectives of the plan. (3)

Sectoral balance of inputs and outputs—each sector must show that its output targets are reasonable in the light of required inputs. (4) There must be a balance of supply and demand at project and sector levels. For an excellent discussion of the ability of Iranian planners to achieve consistency in the drawing up of the Third Plan, see George Baldwin, *Planning and Development in Iran* (Baltimore: Johns Hopkins Press, 1967), chapter 8.

11. Obviously the lack of communication between the Shah and technocrats stems from the social hierarchy of the country in which the Shah has a very special position. Planning in Iran should encourage the Shah and his advisers to think in terms of opportunity costs and to explore direct and indirect effects of policies. There is no indication that this occurs. The case of the Iranian steel industry described by Baldwin, *ibid.*, pp. 107–10, is a typical case in point.

12. Borlin and Looney, *The Battelle Linear Programming Model for Iran*.

13. The model was designed along the lines used by Peter Clark in his *Planning Import Substitution* (Amsterdam: North Holland Publishing Company, 1970).

6

The Surprise-Free Forecast to 2000 A.D.

Introduction

Long-term forecasting of the patterns of development of national economies can be approached in a variety of ways: (1) informed opinion or "guesses," (2) simple extrapolation of past trends, and (3) the generation through an economic model of alternative futures representing different and probable states of the economic system.[1] Extrapolation of past trends is very hazardous for a country undergoing major economic and social transformations; thus the third alternative—the simulation of the economic system under alternative assumptions concerning such variables as oil exports—is undoubtedly the most realistic method of forming a crude picture of the country's future development and thus is the one developed below.

Prospects for Development

At first sight, the prospects of Iran's development appear excellent, yet a realistic forward look at what the economy might become at the end of the century requires an examination of several problems that will face future development and policies in the light of past activity.

Many development problems in Iran are similar to those in other developing nations. Three in particular stand out as important: (1) the problems associated with rapid population growth such as employment creation and the adjustment to urbanization, (2) the ability to absorb efficiently the volume of investment funds needed to sustain high levels of growth, and (3) the progressive transformation of old ways into new. In contrast to most other developing countries, however, Iran's prospects for economic development will continue, as in recent years, to be very closely tied to the development of its oil industry and the efficiency with which the government utilizes these revenues.

Population

The main demographic factors of Iran, as they affect the country's long-run development prospects, are (1) the decrease in the death rate, with the

81

birthrate remaining at a high level, which means that the total population is expanding rapidly, (2) the youthfulness of the population, (3) the rural exodus, and (4) the problem of employment creation.[2]

Population Growth

The population of Iran increased at a low growth rate before 1900, but has increased in subsequent years. At the beginning of the century, it ranged from 6 million to 12 million. Average life expectancy at that time was under 30 years, mainly owing to high infant mortality and lack of health and hygiene facilities. Consequently, the mean age of the population was only about 25 years. At that time the population was growing at an average rate of 0.75 percent annually, although famines, epidemics, and other calamities periodically decimated some regions. Average family size was 4.0 persons, with slight regional variations.[3]

Since 1900 two major population censuses have taken place, the last in 1966 when the total had reached 27.1 million, indicating an average growth rate of 1.54 percent per year in the intervening period. Growth was not constant, however; it was very slow until the 1920s, when transportation for the first time allowed agricultural crops to reach famine regions and thus help to prevent local famines. The rate of population growth then rose from less than 1 percent to 1.5 percent. By the mid-1950s the nationwide spraying of towns and villages against malaria and other endemic diseases, together with additional improvements in health and nutrition standards, helped to overcome high infant mortality and bring the population growth rate up to 2.9 percent per annum.

Between 1956 and 1966 the population grew at an annual rate of about 2.9 percent, and now it is growing at between 2.5 and 3.0 percent; at this rate the population will double in about 23 years. Given that percentage increase annually in the country's population, there will be about 60.7 million[4] Iranians in 2000 A.D. Other assumptions concerning birthrates and fertility rates yield a high of 68.4 million and a low of 56.2 million people in 2000 (Table 6–1).

Age Distribution

The population of Iran is comparatively young;[5] the proportion of those under 15 years of age increased from 42 percent in 1956 to about 47 percent in 1972. This young age structure, together with a mortality rate that is expected to maintain its decline, will tend to sustain the high natural growth rate for at least 10 to 15 years, despite a possible reduction in fertility.

Table 6–1
Projected Population of Iran (per 1000)

	1975	1980	1985	1990	1995	2000
Birthrate						
Rapid decline	40.8	38.5	36.4	33.1	28.9	24.3
Gradual decline	42.8	42.5	42.1	40.8	38.6	36.5
General Fertility of Women (15–44 years)						
Rapid decline	6.12	5.47	4.83	4.18	3.54	2.89
Gradual decline	6.46	6.15	5.84	5.53	5.22	4.91
Population						
Rapid decline	31,900	36,500	41,500	46,700	51,800	56,200
Gradual decline	32,200	37,400	43,700	51,100	59,400	68,400
Steady projection (constant rate)	32,767	37,072	41,943	47,454	53,689	60,744

Source: Compiled by author.

The population problem and its consequences have been recognized by the government, which has been committed to a policy of limiting population growth since 1966. In that year a Deputy Minister for Population and Family Planning was appointed to the Ministry of Health to plan and introduce a national family planning program. The first three years of the program were primarily devoted to establishing an organization with developing awareness of the population problem, and providing services through the facilities of the Ministry of Health. Then, in 1971, the government, recognizing the long-term economic and social effects of a rapid population growth rate, adopted a more aggressive population policy.[6] The declared aim of reducing the annual growth rate to 1 percent by 1991 is desirable but overambitious, given the limited progress made to date.

Geographic Distribution

Twentieth-century changes in the geographic distribution of the population have been in large part related to rural-urban migration. In 1966, about 62 percent (over 15.2 million) of the population lived in rural areas, and 38 percent (over 9.7 million) lived in urban areas (towns and cities with a population of 5000 and over). The corresponding figures for the 1956 census was 69 percent rural (over 13 million) and 31 percent urban (about 5 million). The annual rate of growth of urban population was therefore 6.85 percent—over twice the growth rate of the population as a whole.

Three major factors account for the relative increase in urbanization: (1) the stagnation in the agricultural sector, which has caused a migration to seek employment in the urban areas, (2) the recent rapid growth in industrial development, which offered employment opportunities in urban areas, and (3) the development in communications and transportation, which facilitated the movement of many young ambitious farmers to urban life.

Any projection of the rural-urban distribution of population is necessarily tentative, because it must rest on assumptions about the continuance of past migratory trends and in the light of recent trends that have emphasized a lower rate of population increase in rural than in urban areas. Whereas the overall rate of population growth in Iran was 2.86 percent between 1959 and 1975, the rural population increased at an annual rate of only 1.54 percent while the urban rate of increase was 4.83 percent. Migratory behavior in Iran, as in other Middle Eastern countries, is not fully understood, but it is evident that migratory incentives are not exclusively economic (that is, job-related), but also refer to aspects of social opportunities and at least significant levels of political, intellectual, and other cultural opportunities which are in general greater in urban than in rural areas.

In projecting the urban population, the following factors were taken into account:

1. The age structure of the population and the greater tendency for younger age groups to migrate
2. The past trends in migration from rural to urban areas
3. Transformation of rural communities into urban centers (cities of over 5000).

Based on these considerations, the ratio of urban population to rural should increase rapidly. Beginning in 1972 rural population was a little over 17 million (17.3865 million). By 1980 it is projected to increase to 18.089 million, only to fall to 17.999 million in 1990 and to 17.283 million in 2000. Over the next quarter of a century, therefore, nearly all the increase in the country's population will reside in urban areas.

Employment

In 1956 the economically active[7] population of the country was a little over 6 million (6.07). By 1966 the economically active population had increased to 8.06 million. Between these two years the overall ratio of economically active to total population had declined from 32 percent to 30.8 percent. In 1966, 51.8 percent of all males and 8.6 percent of all females were economically active. The proportion of economically active males is fairly typical by international standards. On the other hand, that of women is much lower than that found in most countries at the same stage of development as Iran. Nevertheless, if the proportion of economically active females in Iran is compared with that of other Islamic countries [for example, Pakistan (1961), 8.8 percent; Syria (1960), 4.2 percent; Morocco (1960), 5.9 percent; the U.A.R. (1960), 4.8 percent], it appears to some extent reasonable.

The most significant characteristic of the distribution of economically active Iranians by age is the high proportion of economically active in the 10–14 and 65+ age groups. The reason for the high level of economic activity among young people is related to two factors: (1) the low age ceiling for compulsory education, and (2) the low legal working age. Although the regulations regarding compulsory education have been in force for a number of years, they have not been fully implemented, especially in rural areas. In addition, the shortage of educational facilities at the primary levels in these areas causes the proportion of rural males in the 10–14 age group attending school to be very small; a high proportion enter the workforce at an early age. The legal working age in Iran is 12 years in contrast to 15 years in most other countries. It is likely, therefore, that expansion of the rural school system and increases in the minimum age will reduce the proportion of economically active in the low age groups. For those 65 and over, participation rates are related to the extension of compulsory social insurance schemes affecting old age and disablement. Since social insurance does not effectively cover many in the 65+ age group and the benefits of retirement pensions are not universally available, many people are obliged to continue to engage in economic and social activity in order to secure their livelihood. With the acceleration of benefits and coverage beginning in the early 1970s, the participation rates in these groups should also fall.

If we assume some decline in the participation of those aged under 14 and over 64 and some increase in the participation of women, this would imply almost no change in the size of the economically active population as a proportion of the working-age population. This would give a little over 18 million economically active in 2000.

While the degree of open unemployment in Iran would appear to be fairly low, or approximately 3.5 percent of the total labor force, it should be noted, however, that these figures are clearly of limited relevance in a situation where only a part of the unemployed workforce is registered. It has been estimated recently that in the rural sector some 40 percent of the total labor force are working less than 42 hours per week, and nearly 15 percent work less than 28 hours per week.[8]

The extent of underemployment of human resources suggested by these figures, which reflect only *visible* unemployment, is supported by a considerable body of indirect evidence relating to low per-head rural incomes, a significant problem of landlessness, chronic nutritional deficiency among the poorest section of rural dwellers, and a high and increasingly costly rate of urban migration.

The magnitude of Iran's future unemployment problem can be appreciated from the fact that the labor force is currently increasing by about 300,000 workers annually. During the Fifth Plan period, the increase in the labor force is likely to be about 1.5 million workers, and given present policies, the prospects for a corresponding increase in employment are not favorable.

A major problem of employment creation has been the failure of the agricultural sector to efficiently absorb additional workers. Despite this, the Fifth Plan has emphasized a strategy of modernization through labor-saving mechanization for the agricultural sector. The implications are clear: mechanization will result in the rate of employment creation in agriculture during the plan period to be close to zero. This would imply the need to absorb both the presently underemployed and the whole of the new addition to the labor force in agriculture during the Fifth Plan in the industrial and services sectors. On the most optimistic assessment, the industrial sector will be able to generate 60,000 to 70,000 jobs per annum over this period. Assuming expansion to continue at its present rate and no change in the marginal capital-labor ratio for this sector, the burden of employment creation will be placed almost entirely on an already swollen urban services sector.

With the present rate of urbanization, unemployment in urban centers would greatly accelerate with serious social and political consequences for the country's prospects of economic growth with social and political stability.

Urban-Rural Income Differences

The extent of potential future underemployment which these figures reveal, though a legitimate cause of concern per se, cannot but suggest more fundamental questions of choice of an appropriate planning strategy for the rest of the century. Iran has been quite fortunate in that it has been possible for the country to finance industrial growth mainly out of oil revenues. The farming areas in the rural sector have, however, not shared in this growth to the extent that a high enough level of expansion of the modern sector could be maintained to sustain a transfer of workforce from the former to the latter. Higher urban incomes have not been passed on directly to the small farmer in terms of higher prices for produce. Changes in the rural-urban terms of trade have, if anything, gone against the rural areas as food prices have been held down by switching foreign exchange from investment to finance food imports while the price of consumer and producer goods to the traditional sector has been allowed to rise, in some cases behind very generous tariff protection.

It could be argued[9] that such a strategy has been necessary to generate the urban-based private savings to finance further rounds of industrial expansion. At the same time, the limits to such a strategy are increasingly apparent. With the exception of the oil sector, Iran's industrial growth has been based almost entirely on import substitution in consumer goods. As such, goods presently account for only about 10 percent of the country's total imports. It is clear that the future import situation will have to concentrate on intermediate and capital goods if growth targets are to be maintained.

A question of key concern is whether such expansion will not be limited by insufficient domestic demand, given the present pattern of income distribution and given, too, the poor prospects for exporting from this sector. In those few capital goods industries where Iran has started to concentrate resources, already present installed capacity is under-utilized and higher tariff protection seems imminent. Protection in this sector, it is clear, would raise costs for the whole of the consumer goods sector; and if present food price policies are pursued, the maldistribution of income from rural and urban sectors, already estimated to be about 6:1 and increasing, would be further accelerated.[10]

The wide gap in rural and urban income differentials is reflected in consumption patterns. For instance, 10 percent of the population at the apex of the income scale accounted in the early 1970s for approximately 40 percent of total private consumption. On the other hand, the 30 percent of the population at the bottom of the income scale accounted for only 8 percent of private consumption. In addition, studies on nutrition have shown that large percentages of both urban and rural families fail to obtain the minimum requirements of calories, protein, and various vitamins.[11] In short, Iran's economy, although growing rapidly, is not yet within sight of being sufficiently developed to generate from within adequate resources to withstand the eclipse of oil. The structure of income and employment and the existence of very real poverty are still indicative of underem-ployment.

Growth

Obviously with higher rates of growth than those anticipated at the time the Fifth Plan was first drawn up, the country will have much more flexibility in solving both its employment and income distribution prob-lems.

One of the major obstacles to determining Iran's ability to sustain high levels of employment and to sustaining high rates of growth for the rest of the century is the basic difficulty of obtaining the proper tableau of the economy with all its interrelationships. Because an economic and social entity such as Iran is very complex, it is impossible to build models capable of reflecting all the interactions necessary for a complete picture of the country's development process. One is left, therefore, with two choices: (1) to build models that are approximations of reality, and (2) to analyze each situation on a partial-equilibrium (all other things being equal) basis. The advantage of the former method is that it enables one to trace back the effects of a change in one or more variables on all the other variables; that is, it provides a method of examining the interactions between a number of important economic variables. The advantage of the latter method is that microproblems or sectoral problems can be exam-ined in great detail and in isolation.

For the purposes of analyzing the country's long-run growth prospects, it is best to choose the first method since the available data from the national income accounts enable econometric estimation of the major macroeconomic interrelationships in the economy.

A Macroeconomic Model for Iran

Our examination of the Iranian economy indicates that the model (a Keynesian[12] or demand approach to the analysis of the country's future growth potential) is theoretically justified and can yield a number of insights into likely constraints on the economy's development; that is, many of the country's current problems result from a lack of adaptation of domestic supply to a changing pattern and level of demand. Under these circumstances, the model can obtain a number of insights into the nature of the mechanisms likely to be at work during the rest of the century.

The relationships in this model indicate the likely state of affairs over time (1972–2000) for different rates of growth of exports and the value added from the oil sector. The model is presented in equation form in Appendix A.

Briefly, the working of the model is as follows: given an assumed rate of export growth, the other components of GNP—consumption, investment, and imports—are determined.

The model has two uses. First, it outlines a procedure for making a first reconnaissance of the growth alternatives confronting the Iranian economy; it provides some criteria for choosing an optimal path among these alternatives. Second, it forms the basis of a Hegelian process designed to examine the probability that the economy will be able to avoid a number of unfavorable trends which are beginning to take on a Marxian tone.

The projections below entail a large number of assumptions. Our approach in this respect has incorporated the following characteristics:

1. In general, we have taken optimistic assumptions with regard to the future. This affects not only our implicit assumptions about such factors as the growth of the world economy and the demand for oil exports, but also elements such as the ability of the government to control domestic inflation.
2. Although there are indications that the Iranian economy may be going through a turning point, and behavioral relationships are shifting in a way that may make some aspects of growth increasingly difficult, we have made optimistic assumptions that the past behavior patterns will hold for the future.

3. We have assumed that the government will continue to play an ever-increasing role in the economy.

Given these assumptions, the model is designed to examine under a surprise-free set of conditions the feasibility of the economy's actually achieving the main objectives of the country. These are:

1. The highest rate of growth permitted by existing resources and the pressing immediate needs of the population
2. The safeguarding of relative price stability within the limits set by the country's institutional constraints and price movements abroad
3. Improvement in the distribution of income, particularly between rural and urban areas

As emphasized before, the forecasts are only the working out of the implications of various assumptions about the economy based on econometric analysis of its key components. As such it is a "surprise-free" forecast.

Projections of Exports

The developments of December 1973, following the Organization of Petroleum Exporting Countries (OPEC) conference, changed radically the world oil situation by quadrupling oil prices and increasing the Iranian government's share of revenues from approximately $1.85 per barrel in early 1973 to approximatey $7.00 per barrel in late 1973. During the latter quarter of 1973 and most of 1974, the government's increase in revenues per barrel was progressively increased to around $10.21 per barrel.

No one can tell with any certainty when Iran's oil revenues will begin to decline in relative or absolute terms, nor when oil will be economically exhausted.[13] Even the figures of known oil reserves seem to be subject to a large margin of error in estimation and to a high probability of revision. The uncertainties are numerous and include not only future production rates, which are to a large extent within the control of Iran, but also changes in the structure and organization of oil producers and consumers, the tactical manipulation of oil supplies by some exporters, the speed with which other sources of energy and fuels become sufficiently competitive, and unpredictable future oil discoveries within and outside Iran.

However, there is every indication that since December 1973, the world has been able to handle the $50 to $60 billion capital flows resulting from oil price increases without major distortions. To a great extent, the oil producers themselves have been aware of the recycling problem and have tried to stem any potential world monetary disorder by substantially increasing their imports of goods and services and by recycling the funds back to the industrialized countries in the form of either loans or direct investments. Such signs of adjustments in the international monetary mechanisms will undoubtedly mean less pressure to lower oil prices, since there is no longer any question of the survival of Western civilization being at stake. Nevertheless, it is clear that the industrialized countries will try to cut their oil imports by introducing energy substitutes, by increasing the efficiency of energy use (cutting waste), and by expanding the search for non-OPEC oil. While the demand for oil is presently sagging, it is not clear to what extent this is a function of the present recessions now afflicting most of the Western industrialized countries, or a function of the efforts brought about to lower oil consumption. Assuming that economic recoveries will be in full swing by 1976, that short-run elasticities of supply are low (a reasonable assumption in view of the implied retooling efforts), and that non-OPEC oil flows will not be substantial, it is not too early to predict a stable but declining demand for OPEC oil. Whether this will translate itself in higher prices will depend on supply and demand conditions as well as on the ability of OPEC to hold together during the confrontation period which seemingly lies ahead.

The model assumes that reserves have once again reached 40 times the current annual production. The figures one obtains upon examining the rate of depletion are still startling. If production continued to rise at 10 percent yearly, half of Iran's estimated reserves would be used up in 11 years' time, with production then reaching nearly 3 times the present level. That is, the then remaining half of the reserves might last another seven years without any further increase in output. If production grew at a cumulative rate of 20 percent per year, only eight years would use up half the estimated reserves, quadrupling annual production and leaving only five more years to exhaust those reserves without further growth in production. These are very short time horizons considering the phenomenal impact oil has on the economy. The present slackening in world demand for oil may make these long-term projections look unrealistic. But Iran appears to be strongly motivated to increase petroleum production; indeed, she managed to raise her exports slightly in 1974 when total OPEC output fell by some 10 percent.

To see a number of different aspects of the economy, the model is simulated under four major assumptions concerning exports (and the value added in oil) that increase at the same rate of 20 percent a year from 1971 to 1975. In model 1 the export rate and the value added in oil decline exponentially to 2000, to give an overall average rate of approximately 10 percent. The same is done in versions 2, 3, and 4 with the rates being 12.5, 15, and 18 percent, respectively. In version 5 the rate of increase in exports and value added in oil is 15 percent from 1970 to 1975, declining exponentially so that the average rate of growth is 5 percent over the period 1972–2000. Each export growth pattern generates a GNP growth rate that, given the exchange rate, produces a foreign trade gap—the difference between exports and imports plus net factor payments. This gap develops as a result of the rapidly expanding demand for imports. The increase in imports with increased GNP is caused by the additional requirements of raw materials and capital goods in the industrial sector and of foodstuffs for consumption. The domestic production of the latter is assumed to be aggravated by rigidities of agricultural supply. At each rate of export growth, another disequilibrium will occur between the amounts of domestic income saved and invested.

Results of the Macroeconomic Model: General Considerations

Given the policy options open to the Iranian government, the forecasts indicate the following:

1. There is general compatibility among most of the economic policy measures as currently used, in the sense that the available policy instruments appear capable of achieving most of the country's major goals. Furthermore, economic policy is potentially consistent in the sense that the policy tools, if used correctly, would exert a favorable impact on the government's goals in the direction desired.
2. A higher rate of economic growth is always associated with a higher growth in exports, but there must be simultaneously an expansion of the private sector.
3. An increase in employment over and above past trends is possible if the economy expands rapidly, and if growth is reoriented toward those activities that are most strongly labor-intensive, such as agriculture.
4. The income distribution between urban and rural areas tends to increase as exports and GNP increase. On the other hand, reorientation of the government's expenditures and the investment of the private sector toward the rural sector can prevent the disparity from becoming increasingly greater.

The qualitative impact of the country's major policy instruments on its main goals is summarized in Table 6–2. The quantitative impacts are presented in Tables 6–3 through 6–7.

Table 6–2
Qualitative Impact of Economic Policy Instruments on Goals

Goals	Instruments				
	Growth Rate	*Reduction in Balance-of-Payments Deficit on Current Account*	*Improved Income Distribution*	*Expanded Employment*	*Reduction of Inflation*
Export Expansion	+	+	–	?	–
Increase in Federal Government Investment	+	?	+	+	–
Increase in Private Investment	+	–	+	+	?
Reorientation of Productive Resources	+	+	+	+	+
Improved Administration of the Public Debt	0	+	0	0	+
General Impact of Instruments on Goals	+	+	?a	+	+

Source: Derived from macromodels.

aDoubtful, although more favorable than if the instruments were not used.

+ Favorable impact
– Unfavorable impact
? Doubtful impact
0 Slight impact, if any

Table 6-3
Iran: Macroeconomic Forecast, 1972–2000, Version 1

Billion 1959 Rials	1972	1976	1980	1985	1990	1995	2000	Average Annual Rate of Growth, Percent
Gross National Product	726.1	1152.4	1714.1	2641.8	3857.3	5277.5	6744.8	8.29
Private Investment	60.2	92.8	145.9	235.8	360.0	521.1	712.5	9.23
Government Investment	88.2	186.5	322.5	545.2	845.6	1217.9	1634.7	10.99
Total Investment	148.4	279.3	468.2	781.0	1205.6	1739.0	2347.2	10.36
Rural Consumption	178.3	192.7	212.1	231.7	256.0	279.2	313.4	2.03
Urban Consumption	268.4	386.1	573.5	872.2	1277.6	1782.3	2348.9	8.06
Total Private Consumption	446.7	578.9	785.6	1103.9	1533.6	2061.6	2662.3	6.58
Government Consumption	123.3	237.5	399.5	658.4	1004.2	1420.7	1867.2	10.19
Total Consumption	570.0	816.4	1185.2	1762.3	2537.8	3482.3	4529.5	7.68
Savings	156.1	336.0	528.9	879.5	1319.5	1795.2	2215.4	9.94
Savings—Investment	7.7	56.7	60.7	98.5	113.9	56.2	-131.8	—
Imports	139.9	283.4	479.6	793.8	1215.3	1732.7	2303.1	10.52
Net Factor Payments	75.2	122.2	187.2	291.9	431.3	598.0	774.9	8.69
Exports	222.9	462.2	727.6	1184.2	1760.5	2386.9	2946.1	9.66
Imports-Exports	-7.8	-56.6	-60.8	98.5	-113.9	-56.2	131.9	—

Source: Computed by author.
Note: Three-year moving averages.

Table 6–4
Iran: Macroeconomic Forecast, 1972–2000, Version 2

Billion 1959 Rials	1972	1976	1980	1985	1990	1995	2000	Average Annual Rate of Growth, Percent
Gross National Product	726.1	1152.4	1935.8	3631.5	6255.6	9513.8	1258.6	10.72
Private Investment	60.2	92.8	155.4	303.8	558.6	919.5	1327.3	11.68
Government Investment	88.2	186.5	373.8	791.4	1453.9	2303.3	3136.8	13.60
Total Investment	148.4	279.3	529.2	1095.2	2012.5	3222.8	4464.1	12.93
Rural Consumption	178.3	192.7	212.9	241.5	290.0	354.2	438.4	3.27
Urban Consumption	268.4	386.1	617.7	1148.1	2016.8	3173.2	4367.3	10.48
Total Private Consumption	446.7	578.9	830.6	1389.6	2306.7	3527.5	4805.7	8.85
Government Consumption	123.3	237.5	440.8	897.3	1632.0	2588.4	3546.9	12.75
Total Consumption	570.0	816.4	1271.3	2286.9	3938.7	6115.9	8352.5	10.06
Savings	156.1	336.0	664.5	1344.6	2316.9	3397.9	4231.1	12.51
Savings—Investment	7.7	56.7	135.3	249.4	304.4	-175.1	-233.0	—
Imports	139.9	283.4	563.8	1181.6	2141.8	3334.9	4442.4	13.15
Net Factor Payments	75.2	122.2	203.7	386.2	679.6	1061.3	1444.4	11.13
Exports	222.9	462.2	902.9	1817.2	3125.6	4571.3	5653.8	12.24
Imports-Exports	-7.8	-56.6	-135.4	-249.4	-304.2	175.1	233.0	—

Source: Computed by author.

Note: Three-year moving averages.

Table 6–5
Iran: Macroeconomic Forecast, 1972–2000, Version 3

Billion 1959 Rials	1972	1976	1980	1985	1990	1995	2000	Average Annual Rate of Growth, Percent
Gross National Product	726.1	1152.4	1895.3	3593.3	6737.6	12129.8	20682.4	12.71
Private Investment	60.2	92.8	153.6	297.8	547.6	1070.0	1891.2	13.10
Government Investment	88.2	186.5	364.8	777.9	1550.4	2890.1	5034.0	15.54
Total Investment	148.4	279.3	518.4	1075.7	2125.0	3816.9	6925.2	14.71
Rural Consumption	178.3	192.7	212.7	240.4	290.7	374.8	528.3	3.96
Urban Consumption	268.4	386.1	609.1	1125.6	2102.0	3816.9	6599.7	12.12
Total Private Consumption	446.7	578.9	821.8	1365.9	2392.8	4191.6	7128.1	10.40
Government Consumption	123.3	237.5	432.4	879.4	1718.6	3180.7	5537.4	14.55
Total Consumption	570.0	816.4	1254.2	2245.4	4113.3	7372.3	12665.5	11.71
Savings	156.1	336.0	641.1	1347.9	2624.3	4757.5	8016.9	15.10
Savings—Investment	7.7	56.7	122.7	272.2	499.3	940.0	1091.7	—
Imports	139.9	283.4	549.1	1161.6	2300.2	4259.1	7362.5	15.21
Net Factor Payments	75.2	122.2	200.4	379.3	714.9	1299.3	2241.3	12.89
Exports	222.9	462.2	872.2	1813.2	3516.4	6355.8	10695.4	14.83
Imports-Exports	-7.8	-56.6	-122.7	-272.3	-501.3	-797.4	-1091.6	—

Source: Computed by author.
Note: Three-year moving averages.

Table 6–6
Iran: Macroeconomic Forecast, 1972–2000, Version 4

Billion 1959 Rials	1972	1976	1980	1985	1990	1995	2000	Average Annual Rate of Growth, Percent
Gross National Product	726.1	1152.4	1982.0	4168.5	9003.2	19259.3	40134.2	15.41
Private Investment	60.2	92.8	156.6	328.8	717.0	1558.7	3308.4	15.38
Government Investment	88.2	186.5	381.7	903.8	2064.7	4542.0	9606.6	18.24
Total Investment	148.4	279.3	538.3	1232.6	2781.7	6100.8	12915.0	17.29
Rural Consumption	178.3	192.7	212.9	244.4	312.1	452.9	764.9	6.22
Urban Consumption	268.4	386.1	623.3	1259.2	2681.4	5737.1	12030.5	14.55
Total Private Consumption	446.7	578.9	836.2	1503.6	2993.5	6190.0	12795.4	12.73
Government Consumption	123.3	237.5	447.1	1004.0	2244.5	4898.9	10348.6	17.14
Total Consumption	570.0	816.4	1283.3	2507.6	5238.0	11088.9	23144.1	14.14
Savings	156.1	336.0	698.7	1660.9	3765.2	8170.4	16990.1	18.23
Savings—Investment	7.7	56.7	160.4	428.3	983.5	2069.6	4075.1	—
Imports	139.9	283.4	576.5	1360.4	3099.0	6796.6	14326.1	17.98
Net Factor Payments	75.2	122.2	206.4	429.5	926.2	1988.8	4169.1	15.42
Exports	222.9	462.2	943.2	2218.3	5008.7	10854.7	22570.3	17.93
Imports-Exports	−7.8	−56.6	−160.3	−428.4	−983.5	−2069.3	−4075.1	—

Source: Computed by author.
Note: Three-year moving averages.

Table 6–7
Iran: Macroeconomic Forecast, 1972–2000, Version 5

Billion 1959 Rials	1972	1976	1980	1985	1990	1995	2000	Average Annual Rate of Growth, Percent
Gross National Product	726.8	1037.6	1317.8	1629.6	1913.2	2133.4	2277.8	4.16
Private Investment	60.2	88.0	123.4	165.6	205.5	241.0	268.8	5.49
Government Investment	88.2	162.8	237.6	321.0	398.1	462.3	506.4	6.44
Total Investment	148.4	250.8	361.0	486.6	603.6	703.3	775.2	6.08
Rural Consumption	178.3	192.3	209.0	219.8	227.7	225.3	224.7	0.83
Urban Consumption	268.4	363.7	476.0	593.2	702.7	794.8	860.5	4.25
Total Private Consumption	446.7	556.0	684.9	813.1	930.3	1020.1	1085.2	3.22
Government Consumption	123.3	215.6	307.8	402.4	489.3	559.6	607.5	5.86
Total Consumption	570.0	771.6	992.8	1215.5	1419.7	1579.7	1692.7	3.96
Savings	156.1	266.0	325.0	414.1	493.5	553.7	585.1	4.83
Savings—Investment	7.7	15.2	−36.0	−72.5	−110.1	−149.6	−190.1	—
Imports	139.9	245.1	347.1	454.6	553.4	633.3	684.2	5.83
Net Factor Payments	75.2	113.3	150.1	188.3	223.3	251.4	270.6	4.68
Exports	222.9	373.6	461.3	570.5	666.6	735.1	764.8	4.50
Imports-Exports	−7.8	−15.2	35.9	72.4	110.1	149.6	190.0	—

Source: Computed by author.
Note: Three-year moving averages.

Obviously a basic assumption in this connection is that the government's policy governing future development, whether it addresses itself to the volume or to the quality of the labor force or to both, will enable the economy to grow at the rates projected above. This growth will not be shared evenly by all sectors, nor will the pattern of national expenditures remain unaltered. Projecting the growth rates of GNP and its major components into industrial origins is even more uncertain. Yet despite the uncertainty of such projections, they do serve the useful purpose of affording a check on the aggregates and furnishing a clearer picture of the total economy with the interrelationships of its major components, as well as more clearly revealing the basic assumptions underlying the projections. Accordingly, the future expenditures consistent with the GNP aggregates are given in Tables 6–3 through 6–7.

Conclusions

The recent developments in the world oil market, following the conclusion of the December 1973 Organization of Petroleum Exporting Countries (OPEC) meeting, have given a new set of constraints to the country's growth. More specifically the quadrupling of crude oil prices suddenly propelled the country from the normal situation for developing countries, that is, constrained by foreign exchange, into an altogether different category. This category is characterized by a capital surplus rather than a capital scarcity.

The models developed here to forecast the likely state of affairs at the end of the century all indicate that the distribution of income in the country tends to become more unequal between the rural and urban sectors as the rate of growth—caused by higher rates of oil exports—increases (Table 6–8). The causes of this distributional pattern are not hard to discern. Increases in government investment go disproportionately into the relatively small urban sector. The best way the country can prevent the income disparity between urban and rural areas from progressively increasing is through upgrading its workforce. The building up of the level of skills cannot move, even under the most favorable conditions, as fast as the capital possibilities occasioned by the flow of oil revenues.

Ironically, therefore, oil revenues have become a mixed blessing for Iran. On the one hand, they are the main determinant of the rate of expansion of the economy, allowing needed investment resources to flow into critical areas necessary for expanding productive capacity; and on the other, if not tightly controlled, they are capable of producing double-digit inflation, a deterioration in the urban-rural income distribution, and

Table 6–8
Iran: Urban-Rural Income Differentials, 1972–2000

Year	Rural Population (millions)	Urban Population (millions)	Ratio of per Capita Urban to Rural Income (Macroeconomic Model)				
			Version 1	Version 2	Version 3	Version 4	Version 5
1972	17.387	12.300	2.129	2.129	2.129	2.129	2.129
1976	17.733	15.035	2.363	2.363	2.363	2.363	2.231
1978	17.910	16.517	2.587	2.602	2.600	2.603	2.318
1980	18.089	18.080	2.705	2.903	2.865	2.929	2.279
1982	18.089	19.912	2.816	3.235	3.170	3.328	2.233
1985	18.089	22.833	2.982	3.765	3.711	4.081	2.138
1987	18.089	24.905	3.077	4.084	3.990	4.644	2.073
1990	17.999	28.301	2.174	4.424	4.599	5.465	1.963
1992	17.819	30.825	3.21	4.533	4.873	5.925	1.890
1995	17.553	34.831	3.212	4.514	5.133	6.383	1.816
1997	17.380	37.656	3.182	4.390	5.189	6.502	1.778
2000	17.293	41.975	3.088	4.104	5.146	6.480	1.573

Source: Compiled from Tables 6–3 through 6–7.

undesirable concentrations of individual wealth. All these adverse effects are theoretically manageable in that planners can divide oil revenues into either domestic or external investment activities; that is, the oil revenues can be used as foreign exchange reserves or can be sent abroad in the form of foreign investments. Needless to say, efficient management and planning under the existing conditions of capital surplus requires a shift of emphasis within planning circles from an allocation of resources to simply increase growth in the short run to one of maximizing over a fairly long time horizon the potential for the economy to achieve self-sufficiency, and at the same time minimizing the disruptive effects that the revenues may create.

The major policy issue in the field of economic development facing Iran in the immediate future is how to absorb efficiently its surplus oil revenues. The financing of a program of development, in alignment with the government's policy of maintaining high rates of economic growth, does not seem to constitute a major problem or precipitate a crucial bottleneck in the immediate future, as long as oil revenues continue to flow in in substantial volumes. No major problems are expected to arise either with domestic prices or with the external balance of payments. Eventually, of course, other sources of finance, particularly taxation and surplus returns on government enterprise (steel, aluminum, and so on), must supplement, and in time replace, oil revenues.

Final Observations

In this context it is distressing to note that as of this writing (August 1976) Iran has already overextended its budget and has been forced to begin borrowing in the Euromarkets. The government is already short of cash as a result of overspending, particularly on military equipment. As a matter of policy, the Shah has allocated at least one-half of each year's oil revenues to military expenses.[14] All told, Iran has placed orders for more than $10 billion worth of military equipment from the United States alone since early 1972, and Iran announced in early August 1976 that it planned a total of $10 billion worth of military purchases from the United States from 1975 through 1980.

In early 1976 the Shah declared that several large-scale purchases could be made only if they were in the form of barter deals involving Iranian oil that would otherwise remain unsold. The United States government, in turn, has taken the position that arms sales of this magnitude to Iran are justified as part of the implementation of the 1969 Nixon Doctrine, which basically recommended that regional leaders such as the Shah assume greater responsibility for security in their areas; that is, it suited United States interests to have a strong Iran capable of defending itself.[15] Unless Iran can control its urge to spend on military arms, the forecasts made concerning the country's improving prosperity by the end of the century will obviously be academic exercises.

Notes

1. A detailed description of the forecasts that have been made within each category is given in Oskar Morgenstern, Klaus Knorr, and Klaus Heiss, *Long Term Projections of Power: Political, Economic, and Military Forecasting* (Cambridge, Mass.: Ballinger Publishing Co., 1973), part II.

2. J. Behnam, "Population," in W. B. Fischer, ed., *The Cambridge History of Iran: Volume I—The Land of Iran* (Cambridge: Cambridge University Press, 1968), p. 483.

3. Julian Bharier, *Economic Development in Iran 1900–1970* (New York: Oxford University Press, 1971), chapter 1.

4. These forecasts are roughly in line with other projections. See, for example, *Past Population Trends and Future Forecast of Iran Population up to 1991* (Tehran: Iranian Statistical Center, 1971), mimeo. For 1991 the Center has a high forecast of 54.4 million and a low forecast of 46.2 million. Population and Manpower Bureau, Planning Division, *Iran's Population—Past, Present and Future* (Tehran: Plan and Budget Organization, 1973). For 1991 this study has a high forecast of 55.8 million and a low of 50.1 million people. Family Planning Unit, *Projection of Iran's Population* (Tehran: Ministry of Health, 1968). This forecast gives a high of 63.4 million for 1991 and a low of 45.6 million people.

5. Unless otherwise specified, the population and employment data have been obtained from *The First Census of Iran* (Tehran: The Ministry of Interior, November 1966); and National Statistical Center, *National Census of Population and Housing* (Tehran: Plan Organization, March 1968).

6. An excellent description of Iran's family planning programs is outlined in Richard Moore et al., "Population and Family Planning in Iran," *Middle East Journal* 396–408, Autumn 1974. They indicate that the experience of the government program to date points to the need to place far more emphasis on information and educational activities. The evidence they present suggests that a major reason for low contraceptive continuation rates, clinic underutilization, and other factors that mitigate clinic effectiveness may be the general lack of information about and the low confidence in the idea of changing fertility behavior. They conclude

that although Iran's rapid socioeconomic progress will probably tend automatically to change this over time, the many pronatalist forces will tend to keep fertility far higher in the short run than that desired by economic and social planners (Moore et al., *ibid.*, p. 407).

7. "Economically active" is defined in the official censuses by the "gainful worker for the size of labor." Based on this concept, all persons who were employed at any time during the seven days preceding the numerator's visit, the seasonally unemployed, and those who were unemployed but seeking employment were considered economically active. The economically inactive group consisted of homemakers, students, those unable to work, and others. Cf. references in note 5 above.

8. This is the definition of unemployment given by the International Labor Organization in *Employment and Income Policies for Iran* (Geneva, 1973), chapter 3.

9. This is based on a "Cambridge" savings function relationship developed by N. Kaldor, "A Model of Economic Growth," *Economic Journal* (December 1957). There is no indication that the financial markets in Iran are so underdeveloped that all savings must come out of profits. For a current evaluation of the Iranian financial markets, see Abolghasem Kheradjou, "Banking Structure," Gunter Rischer, "The Stock Exchange," and Medhi Samii, "Banking Growth," in *Euromoney* (May 1975).

10. Cf. Harry Oshima, "Income Distribution," working paper for the International Labor Organization report on employment in Iran, Tehran, 1972 (mimeo).

11. *Ibid.*

12. For a critique and similar conclusion to the applicability of Keynesian models for Iran, cf. Firouz Vakil, "An Econometric Model for Iran," *Bank Markazi Iran Bulletin* **11**, 1972, pp. 115–120; "An Econometric Model for Iran: Estimated Structural Equations," *Bank Markazi Iran Bulletin*, **12**, 1973, pp. 633–655; and *Determining Iran's Financial Surplus 1352–1371—Some Management Concepts* (Tehran: The Institute for International Political and Economic Papers, 1975).

13. Some speculative forecasts of demand are given by C. Blitzer et al., "A Dynamic Model of OPEC Trade and Projection," B. A. Halmon, "Economic Incentives in OPEC Oil Pricing Policy," and D. Fischer et al., "The Prospects for OPEC: A Critical Survey of Models of the World Oil Market," all in *Journal of Development Studies* (December 1975). The assumptions in these models do not differ significantly from the ones made in this study.

Forecasts of reserves are, of course, always hazardous because of new discoveries. An excellent account of the country's continued search for additional deposits of petroleum is given in Fereidun Fesharaki, *Development of the Iranian Oil Industry* (New York: Praeger Publishers, 1976). To give an idea of the difficulty of the problem the country currently faces, Iran's oil reserves were estimated in 1970 to be 40 times that year's production level. Production rose by 18.4 percent in 1971, 9.8 percent in 1972, and again by 18 percent in 1973. Using the 1970 figures, we might deduce that by the end of 1973 reserves were only 27 times the annual production rate. However, besides the possibility of discovering new reserves, a rise in oil prices (as has been occurring generally) brings an increase in estimated reserves since a greater quantity of oil can be profitably extracted from any given oil field. This adjustment of reserves is extremely difficult to quantify. Cf. Kamal Aammeed and Margaret Bennett, "Iran's Future Economy," *The Middle East Journal* 418–20, 1975.

14. For a detailed breakdown of the types of weapons and expenditures incurred, cf. Robert Looney, "Iran: The Rise of a World Power," *Countermeasures*, May 1975.

15. This was stressed in Secretary of State Kissinger's recent trip to Iran. Cf. *The New York Times*, August 12, 1976, p. 11.

7

**Limitations of the Delphi
Method for Planning
in Iran and a
Hegelian Alternative**

Introduction

The surprise-free forecast to the year 2000 has, because of falling oil demand and the country's accelerating imports, largely consisting of military equipment, already given an inaccurate picture of the country's long-run growth prospects. Iran is currently floating bonds[1] in the Euromarkets and as of this writing (August 1976) is seriously short of foreign exchange. Despite their poor predictive ability, however, long-run forecasts are still a valuable planning exercise in Iran. Obviously, it is easy for a highly critical Iranian (or other reader) to grant them entertainment value only. In fact, studies of this type (like *The Year 2000*,[2] for example) are valuable because they summarize conveniently, and interrelate interestingly, a great deal of current knowledge and expectations; that is, they shed valuable insights into the process by which nations such as Iran start to sustain a process of economic growth and if that growth falters, indicate what government officials and planners might be able to do to reverse any undesirable trends. These forecasts identify a range of eventualities that are not obvious, but may in fact be possible. They provide a framework for productive policy implementation.

Yet even on the rather simple level of venturing informal guesses about the future, long-range forecasts still do not enter into the decision-making process in Iran. Obviously, the Shah and his advisers do not think them useful. Undoubtedly, information of this nature, by itself, does not permit all the officials to deal directly with the major problems facing the country as they see them.

Planning in Iran is still primarily directed toward simple short-run (five-year) forecasts of the economy, with an occasional twenty-year forecast being made.[3] In rare situations such as the Battelle model, short-run models attempting to optimize growth or consumption during a short period (usually five years) and within a well-defined context are also constructed. Therefore planners in Iran have devoted most of their energy toward somewhat irrelevant (to the politicians) problems. The major reason the Plan and Budget Organization had no real influence over the decision-making process in Iran is that most of the problems faced by the Shah and his aides are not well structured, nor are the issues government officials must deal with constant over time.

To be taken seriously, therefore, planners in Iran must spend less time perfecting such techniques as linear programming and devote more energy to determining the government's underlying needs for planning. This requires that the planners ascertain the underlying assumptions concerning the goals that the Shah and his advisers wish to see achieved at various points in time. In doing so the planners would form a picture concerning the country's future development process from the point of view of the authorities. Through this process of discerning the authorities' needs and priorities, the PBO would be stimulated into adopting a broader and more relevant view of the country's economic requirements.

While the process of constructing a new planning framework will be exceedingly complicated, its characteristics are fairly easy to specify:[4]

1. The approach must be concerned with future states of the country, and hence predictions must be made about them.
2. The planning process must be capable of identifying and selecting an optimal development path based on the underlying value judgments of the Shah and other high officials; that is, it must enable them to achieve certain ends.
3. It must be capable of presenting a choice from two or more plans for the country's policy makers.

It is important to note that each of these items involves an articulation of both the planners' and officials' basic assumptions about the country's development process.

In Iran these assumptions involve a definition of such items as (1) the desirable growth rate over time, (2) the time phasing of consumption and investment, (3) the regional distribution of growth, (4) the income distribution, (5) the rate of inflation, and so on. In fact, the approach taken toward planning must be capable of incorporating all relevant sociopolitical economic considerations that may require action from the officials at any time to steer the economy back toward the desired development path (as defined by the authorities).

The Delphi Method

A logical starting point in constructing a new framework for economic policy making in Iran would be to utilize a number of the so-called experts that have been so critical of the mathematical techniques developed for planning by the PBO. A number of techniques capable of minimizing the purely mathematical and mechanistic aspects of forecasting for planning needs are available.[5] For example, a variety of the Delphi[6] method could be used to predict and forecast 10 to 25 years ahead in areas considered to be in the national interest, that is, future energy demands, weapon systems, the national transportation requirements, and so on. The Delphi approach toward making these forecasts would involve a sequence of questionnnaires to experts in each area of specialization. A summary of their predictions from each round of questionnaires could then be fed back to the respondents before they execute another succeeding round of questionnaires.

The Delphi method would therefore depend on a group of experts (presumably Iranian) making forecasts, which in turn would be formulated separately (that is, shunning the committee method that is now used in the Economic Council and in the Plan and Budget Organization), revised by them in the light of responses of other experts, and roughly aggregated by the Director of the Plan and Budget Organization, for example.

Advocates of this approach[7] claim that predictions derived in this manner would lessen the chance of unanticipated events and thus provide the government with a sounder basis for long-range decision making than the forecasts currently made by the PBO, or for that matter than the purely intuitive judgments that in practice are the basis upon which current planning decisions in the country are made.

On first examination there are two reasons to believe that the Delphi method would seem to offer planners in Iran a strong tool from which to upgrade the quality and political acceptability of the PBO's development plans. First, information derived from the Delphi surveys would provide judgmental input data for use in the social science area. This is an area in which hard data in Iran are unavailable or too costly to obtain. For instance, a major study of socioeconomic strategies for developing the country in the 1972–1977 period was begun in the preliminary stages of drawing up the Fifth Plan, but was soon abandoned because of the lack of statistics in that area. The second advantage presented by the Delphi method is its use of expert opinions among the nation's intellectual community—a group that has not for some reason participated actively in the country's planning process.

The use of the Delphi method to supply data in the social sciences and to provide decision makers with ready access to specialized expertise are of great potential importance in Iran.

Overall, however, two major limitations exist in the use of the Delphi methodology of forecasting in Iran. First, this Delphi method still lacks a completely sound theoretical basis. This is due largely to the fact that Delphi, by definition, is concerned with the utilization of experts' opinions and that experts willing to be used essentially as experimental laboratory subjects are rarely available in Iran. The use of the method would therefore be confined to studies carried out without proper experimental controls or from controlled experiments in which students are used as surrogate experts.

For these reasons it is quite unlikely that, from a purely technical standpoint, the Delphi method could be used in Iran in a manner usually applied to problems in the more developed countries. More fundamentally, however, the limitations for use in Iran of the Delphi method are political: the "experts" or students who would be needed for the analyses would probably not be acceptable to the country's rulers.

The professional, bureaucratic intelligentsia needed for the Delphi method is a new class in Iran. It is composed primarily of individuals whose power position rests upon employment that utilizes those skills and talents which they have attained through their modern education. This is a nonbourgeois middle class, many of whose members consider a successful career to be based on performance and service, in contrast to the average Iranian who envisages the road to position and/or status through material wealth, family ties, or property.[8] The members of the intellectual class are engaged largely in professional, technical, cultural, teaching, and administrative occupations, and are generally salaried middle class. They are distrusted by the Shah for obvious reasons—members of this group have organized most of the assassination plots against him and in general have been "troublemakers."

Many of the intellectuals in Iran, while teachers at either Tehran University or other universities, have been attached on a full- or part-time basis to the PBO.[9] The ministries and other agencies are beginning to attract competent economists, but their staffs are still predominated by nontechnically oriented administrators. The two groups, the intellectuals and administrators, have mutual contempt and suspicion. This conflict is reflected in constant bickering and behind-the-scenes maneuvering. Moreover, it is no secret that a number of ex-Tudeh (that is, communist) party members are in the PBO; the Shah has boasted[10] of this as an example of his clemency. Be that as it may, these individuals and certain other intellectuals (who are probably not communists) in the PBO are committed to rational planning, that is, strictly economic approaches to planning as a means of introducing, through such means as a more equitable distribution of income, a rapid rate of social change in Iran. Their concern with equity and income distribution has often antagonized the more politically conservative (usually found in the ministries) and thus further intensifies the intellectual-administrative antagonism that is beginning to divide the country.

For example, in the early 1960s a number of incidents of major proportion occurred in the streets of Tehran as the professional middle class led rallies, riots, and demonstrations. Students and teachers were the major participants.[11] In January 1960, 3 students were killed and 50 injured in riots protesting tightened examination rules. In May 1961, during demonstrations demanding higher pay, one teacher was killed and two were injured. The following January (1962), picketing students demanded free elections and the resignation of Premier Amini. Then 1 student was killed, 200 were injured, and some 300 persons were arrested as Iranian commandos invaded Tehran University. The University itself has been closed many times since those incidents by students and teachers.

On April 10, 1965, an attempt was made on the Shah's life. Fourteen young men were subsequently brought to trial for complicity in what has come to be called the Marble Palace Plot. The accused men, who averaged 27 years of age, were all members of the middle-class intelligentsia. In 1968, fourteen members of the intelligentsia were apprehended and charged with communist ideological leanings and conspiracy; all were university men, and their average age was 29. In early 1971, eighteen young men were sentenced and imprisoned for "antistate activities." Among the members of this group were twelve students, three civil servants, and a pharmacist; their average age was 25. In January 1972, the Iranian government announced the discovery of three extensive networks of individuals who were plotting antistate terrorist activities against the regime. Subsequently, a number of other groups have been apprehended. An examination of the members of these groups indicates that once again the professional intelligentsia was assuming its place at the forefront of the alienated opposition.

Even more fundamental is the distrust accorded the intelligentsia by the Shah and other top politicians—a distrust related to this group's general outlook and set of values:[12]

1. They refuse to accept the traditional power relationships that dominate Iranian society. As such, they pose a threat to the ongoing political system.

2. They possess superior educations, as opposed to the traditional, religious-oriented, rote-learning education possessed by the older administrator politicians.

3. They have been exposed in varying degrees to outside philosophies, thoughts, and ideas. They have an awareness and an open-mindedness to alien systems of thought—a profound switch from the tradition-bound members of the old elite class. Their great and sudden awareness of other sociopolitical systems and philosophies has been dramatic. Marxian philosophy often dominates the thinking of the intelligentsia.

4. They are free of any rigid religious dogmatism and of any blind worship of past history. In fact, that which is sacred to the more traditional middle class is either ignored or attacked by this group. They are little impressed by either Iran's history or its prophets.

Because of the threat this group poses to the Shah, their advice would be unacceptable to him. In fact, they are beginning to pose a real problem for his government. Their growth has profound implications in terms of the country's future political system and the process of change. The middle class has created new relationships, demands, and imbalances which will in large part determine the future of Iran.

The Shah's, and hence the government's, world view is a product of Iran's sociopsychological environment. The fundamental predictions, values, and criteria for choosing means to implement the Shah's plans are deeply rooted vestiges of his cultural heritage. Through his experience the Shah has developed habitual ways of viewing the country and coping with its (and often his associated) problems. The country's poorly conceived development plans have served only to reinforce his deep suspicion of the intelligentsia and technocratic groups. Yet the complexities of the country's growth are becoming so great that he needs the expertise of these groups.

The Shah's problem is similar to one described in a somewhat different context by J. K. Galbraith,[13] that of the information process in large American corporations. Galbraith's position is that the conventional argument made by most economists, that is, that the owners or managers of large corporations are in a position of control, is false. It is the technostructure that has control. The technostructure, according to Galbraith, extends from the most senior officials of the corporation at the outer perimeter to the white- and blue-collar workers whose function is to conform more or less mechanically to instruction or routine. It embraces all who bring specialized knowledge, talent, or experience to group decision making. This, not the management, is the guiding intelligence, the brain, of the enterprise. The point is that if decision requires the combined information of a group, it cannot be safely reversed by an individual. In short, effective power of decision is lodged deeply in the technical, planning, and other specialized staff.[14]

Fortunately, it is possible to design a planning framework that would allow the Shah and his aides to benefit from the technocrats' insights and technical capabilities without necessarily being dependent upon them, in the sense that these officials would not be able to verify or understand the basic assumptions upon which the final forecasts used in planning were made. This methodology is based on Hegelian or dialectical[15] analysis.

The Hegelian system[16] begins with the premise that every set of propositions that can be made about an economy is simply a reflection of a more general theory or plan about the nature of the development process as a whole system, that is, a world view. This being the case, some alternative and sharply differing world view exists that would permit the serious consideration of an opposite set of propositions concerning the development process. The question that the Shah and his aides would have to face when presented this argument by the intelligentsia is why this opposite view might not be true or more desirable than their own. Further, the Shah might be in a better position to determine whether the conflict between his plan and the counterplan might not allow a third plan or world view to be constructed that would be a creative synthesis of the original plan and the counterplan.

A Hegelian Approach to Development Planning in Iran

A system is Hegelian if it examines a situation completely and logically from two different points of view. In the case of Iran, the Hegelian approach would begin by examining the prevailing or recommended PBO plan and the data used to derive it. In the debate between the Shah (with his aides) and the PBO planners, the authorities would first ask the planners under what view of the world is the PBO plan the "optimal" one to follow. In the process of examining the reasoning used in drawing up the plan, the intelligentsia and technocrats would begin articulating the basic assumptions that underlie their plan. That is, this questioning process between the Shah and PBO would serve to interpret the data so as to conclude logically that this plan is best for achieving the leader's goals.

To fully test the assumptions underlying the PBO plan, another plausible and believable alternative—the Shah's counterplan—must then be presented. This counterplan (as with the plan) should have the attributes of being feasible, politically viable, and generally credible to the populus. The view of the world for which the counterplan is optimal is then determined in the same manner as above, through a structured discourse between the Shah and PBO officials.

The principal theme of the Hegelian process is that the authorities learn about the fundamental assumptions of the country's planning problem and come to understand them by observing the conflict between the PBO plan, their counterplan, and the attendant world views that underlie each. The vehicle for inducing this reflection is a structured debate.

The structured debate, contrary to the PBO's voluminous planning document or the traditional briefing before the Economic Council, would consist of the most forceful presentation possible of the two opposing plans, given that each side must utilize the same set of data concerning socioeconomic conditions in the country. As a possible format, the structured debate could take place before the Economic Council and would begin with the advocate of the PBO plan stating his world view or model of the situation. Advocates of the counterplan would follow the same procedure. Then, as each item of data were introduced, it would be utilized by the opposing side (the authorities) in a manner that would best support their plan and negate the opponent's plan. The process of analysis and counteranalysis of the opposed plans would continue until all the reliable data bearing on the country's development problems had been considered.

In Hegelian terminology, the plan (thesis) is opposed by the counterplan (antithesis), both of which are constructed and argued for from the same data bank (the essence). Hegel's theory leads us to predict that the Shah—observer of the conflict—will integrate and form a new and expanded world view (the synthesis). The synthesis includes exposing hidden assumptions and developing a new conceptualization of the planning problem the country faces.

Conditions for the Employment of the Hegelian System

The Hegelian approach to development planning in Iran presupposes four conditions which, if they are currently present in the government bureaucracy, would make the Hegelian method a marked improvement over the current planning process. They are:

1. The Shah and other politicians must be unaware of some important assumptions underlying the PBO's models of the economy and are thus in doubt as to both the appropriate assumptions to adopt and the particular plan or approach to the country's development to choose; that is, there is no basic agreement on assumptions between the Shah and the advisers (the PBO).
2. The government must acknowledge that multiple interpretations of the data exist concerning the country's major economic variables, each of which would indicate a different approach in terms of the optimal planning strategy for the country.
3. The Hegelian method is amenable to cases of decision making under uncertainty. In situations of uncertainty, the government can look to the PBO for estimates of the magnitude of uncertainty or the key assumptions upon which forecasts are made (thus deducing the degree of uncertainty instead of, as is now the case, "absorbing" the uncertainty inherent in the situation). Thus, in the Hegelian model, the PBO can communicate different conclusions that are derived from different assumptions. The Shah and his advisers can then rely on their judgment to formulate a synthesized set of assumptions upon which the validity of his ultimate choice of development plans will depend.

The Hegelian System: Basic Methodology

The Hegelian system used for the long-run forecasts in this study (Chapter 9) is based on two assumptions: (1) Truth is elusive; that is, the understanding of the Iranian economy can result only from a highly complicated analysis which depends on the identification of a planned chain of events and a diametrically opposed counterplanned chain of events. The plan and the counterplan represent strongly divergent and opposing conceptions of how to manage the economy. The plan and the counterplan then must engage each other in an unremitting debate over the "true" nature of the whole system until a new plan emerges that reconciles, synthesizes, and encompasses the plan and the counterplan. (2) Data discussed out of context are meaningless and only become useful information by being coupled to the plan and the counterplan; that is, the data alone support neither plan. The Hegelian system assumes that without both the plan and the counterplan, there is no way to interpret the implications of the country's socioeconomic data.

Conclusions

The Hegelian methodology suggested for planning in Iran would incorporate at least two antithetical representations of the problem. It would begin with either the prior identification or the creation of two strongly opposed models of the problem. These opposing representations would illustrate the underlying opposed assumptions regarding the theoretical nature of the problem. Both of these representations would then be applied to the same socioeconomic statistical base in order to demonstrate the crucial nature of the underlying theoretical assumptions of both positions. In theory, the same set of data could be used to support either the PBO's or the Shah's view of the planning problem. Out of the Hegelian confrontation between the opposing interpretations of the country's development problems, the underlying assumptions of both would be brought up to the surface for examination by the decision maker (the Shah). It is hoped that as a result of witnessing the dialectical confrontation between the experts of each side, the government officials will be in a better position to form their own view, and thus achieve not only a better utilization of the country's technical experts but a general upgrading of the country's economic policy making.

Notes

1. Ludwig Poullain, "The Major Borrowers on the International Capital Markets This Year," *Euromoney*, 3–6, February 1976.

2. Herman Kahn and Anthony Weiner, *The Year 2000: A Framework for Speculation on the Next Thirty-Three Years* (New York: Macmillan, 1967).

3. A notable exception is Planning Division, Planometrics Bureau,

A Twenty Year Macro-Economic Perspective for Iran, 1351–1371 (Tehran: Planning Division, PBO, May 1974), mimeo.

4. A number of requirements are possible. For an excellent discussion of related issues, see W. Arthur Lewis, *Development Planning: The Essentials of Economic Policy* (New York: Harper and Row, 1966), especially chapter 1.

5. Cf. Oskar Morgenstern et al., *Long Term Projections of Power: Political, Economic, and Military Forecasting* (Cambridge, Mass.: Ballinger Publishing Co., 1973), chapter 4.

6. The Delphi method is excellently summarized in a number of papers in Harold Linstone and Murray Turoff, eds., *The Delphi Method: Techniques and Applications* (Reading, Mass.: Addison-Wesley Publishing Co., 1975).

7. For example, Robert Decker, "Future Economic Developments: A Delphi Survey," *Futures*, 142, April 1974.

8. Norman Jacobs, *The Sociology of Development: Iran as a Case Study* (New York: Praeger Publishers, 1966), chapter 6.

9. George Baldwin, *Planning and Development in Iran* (Baltimore: Johns Hopkins Press, 1967), chapter 7.

10. Mohammed Reza Shah Pahlavi, *Mission for My Country* (London: Hutchinson, 1961), p. 106.

11. As described by James Hill, *The Politics of Iran: Groups, Classes and Modernization* (Columbus, Ohio: Charles Merrill, 1972), pp. 139–42.

12. As described in James Hill, "The Plasticity of Informal Politics: The Case of Iran," *The Middle East Journal,* 131–51, Spring 1973.

13. J. K. Galbraith, *The New Industrial State* (Boston: Houghton Mifflin, 1967).

14. The Galbraith ideas are reviewed in depth by Myron Sharpe, *John Kenneth Galbraith and the Lower Economics* (White Plains, N.Y.: International Arts and Sciences Press, Inc., 1972); and James Meade, "Is the New Industrial State Inevitable?" *Journal of Political Economy*, June 1968. The interested reader should particularly consult Robert Solow and J. K. Galbraith, "The New Industrial State: A Discussion," *Public Interest*, Fall 1967.

15. A complete survey of the dialectical method is given in Lyn Marcus, *Dialectical Economics* (Lexington, Mass.: D.C. Heath, 1975).

16. References to Hegel's system are taken from *Great Works of the Western World, Hegel* (Chicago: Encyclopedia Britannica, 1952); and Georg Wilhem Hegel, *The Philosophy of History* (New York: John Wiley & Sons, Inc., 1944).

8

A Hegelian-Marxian Analysis of the Economy

Introduction

The Shah has over the years prided himself on his place in history, his most important accomplishment being the halt of a Communist takeover in the early 1950s. He often refers to the importation of Marxian ideas into the country. For example, in a major speech[1] (May 2, 1975) marking the beginning of a one party system in Iran, the Rastakhiz Party,[a] the Shah asked a rhetorical question: "Why did the idea of this national political structure occur to me on February 11, 1974?" Ironically he noted that this intitiation of a new form of government occurred while the country was at the peak of its success, was going forward, and in his words was "regularly achieving its ambitious aims." He noted that the timing of this move was finally at hand because a number of Marxist parties and elements had finally been subdued and that now all elements of the population could participate in the political process.

In other contexts the Shah has repeatedly referred to his Prime Minister in the early 1950s, Mossadegh, as a Marxist. In his book, *Mission for My Country*,[2] the Shah noted that during Mossadegh's administration in 1952 and 1953, when the Tudeh (the Iranian Marxist party) and other mobs increasingly terrorized the capital and other leading cities, Mossadegh did virtually nothing to stop them.[3] With the fall of Mossadegh and after a period of consolidation, the Shah in his same May 1975 speech noted that with the Sixth Bahman 1341 (January 26, 1963), he was finally able to consult the nation directly. This development, according to the Shah, came after the sorrowful and bitter World War II years, military occupation, the establishment of treacherous and fake (Marxist) parties, intellectual degeneration, the continuation of feudalism, and the exploitation of some by other Iranians.

The Shah noted that the White Revolution initiated by him on the Sixth Bahman 1341 drew a united response from the nation, largely because his "revolution from above" was basically aimed at the liberation of Iranian farmers, who constituted more than 75 percent of the country's total population, thus meaning in essence the freedom of the majority of Iranians from slavery or a condition close to it, or as the farmers themselves put it, their "rebirth."

---

[a]Roughly translated, the Rastakhiz Party means the National Resurgence Party.

A Marxian View of Change in Iran

It was apparent to the Shah (as it would have been to Marx if he were alive) that the country was on the verge of a revolution in the 1950 and early 1960 period. As Marx[4] had observed, the great revolutions of European history occurred as a violent response on the part of one class which, while becoming predominant in economic activity, found itself impeded in achieving its economic potential by the obsolete but still ruling class.[5] As illustration, Marx believed he was witnessing in 1848 a contest for power between a rising bourgeois class and Germany's political institutions appropriate to a bygone age. Monarchy represented, in Marx's view, a medieval vestige. The laws and institutions of this class stifled the economic advancement of the bourgeois. The conflict between the classes eventually became so great that the bourgeois had to seize power.

Revolutions of the type described by Marx, that is, class revolutions, have been delayed by clever maneuvering by those in power. In fact, European history is replete with examples of monarchs such as the Shah who have attempted to stave off a revolution by seeking allies against the aristocracy (in Iran they are mainly landowners). At the same time they have been threatened by the rise of the bourgeois middle class. In Europe the monarchs often allied themselves against their own nobility as well as curtailed the immediate threat of the middle class. Most of these attempts were unsuccessful. The few successful examples of "revolution from above" occurred when the ruling monarch or elite formed an alliance with the middle class by making basic concessions to the expanding new class. The Shah's revolution is interesting precisely because he has formed an alliance not with the middle classes but with the lower classes. His strategy seems to be based on curtailing the power not only of the aristocracy but of the expanding middle class.

The White Revolution represents, therefore, a new attempt calculated by the Shah to introduce reform from above, a reform that in the end will be capable of preserving the country's traditional power patterns. Through land reform the Shah has managed to reduce the power of the aristocracy by severing their connection with the countryside. He then moved to ally himself with the peasantry against the professional middle class. His basic strategy was similar to one described by Marx; that is, it was designed to buttress his position by weakening the opportunity for upper-class challengers.

The great threat to his power, however, is now posed by the professional, bureaucratic intelligentsia. The Shah had hoped to gain the support of the peasants against this class, and it was in this spirit that the land reform program became the focal point of the White Revolution.

In total, there are twelve major reforms included within the Shah's White Revolution.

1. Redistribution of land among the peasants
2. Nationalization of forests and pastures
3. Sale of shares in government factories
4. Profit sharing for workers
5. The enfranchisement of women
6. Formation of the Literacy Corps (military conscripts teaching in villages)
7. Formation of the Health Corps (military conscripts as rural paramedics and santiation teachers)
8. Formation of the Extension and Development Corps
9. Establishment of Equity Courts (rural justice system relying on arbitration and common law)
10. Nationalization of water
11. Urban and rural reconstruction
12. Reform of the governmental administration edifice and education

The first six reforms were initiated in 1963, the following three in 1964, the final three in 1967. In practice, as one stage was achieved, the reform was taken to a new level. By this means, the Shah hoped to achieve a permanent state of what he has termed "revolutionary reform."

In general the members of the Iranian professional middle class resent what they believe to be a deliberate attempt by the Shah to exclude them from the White Revolution. Obviously none of the twelve points is directly related to them; that is, none of their demands for fundamental change in the political system have been addressed, and their hopes for improvements in such fundamental areas as educational reform and social justice have been omitted from the revolution.[6]

Their complaints have been dismissed by the politicians on the grounds of the intelligentsia's stupidity, conceit, negativism, and individualism. A wide gap currently separates the professional middle class and the political elite. The latter often label the intelligentsia "a threat to the revolution." Yet the same political elite recognizes that the participation of the new class is essential to the success of the land reform program. The politicians and most of the older bureaucrats do not have the technical skills to implement many rural programs essential to the success of the White Revolution. The politicians have therefore become increasingly dependent on the intelligentsia for the preservation of the revolution.

The whole process has led to increasing cynicism; many of the intelligentsia view government employment as simply a temporary bribe to obtain their support. Certain circles of Iranian scholars go so far as to describe the entire program as "bribery of the intellectuals." The White Revolution is viewed by them in terms of an obvious attempt to turn the peasant against the professional middle class and in the long run enable the Shah to preserve the nation's semifeudal socioeconomic political system, that is, the 2500-year monarchy. Marx would certainly have had some acid comments concerning the Shah's attempts at self-preservation.

The Iranian Revolution

The programs and reforms introduced as integral parts of the White Revolution have created a number of far-reaching consequences that were not foreseen by the Shah or other members of the ruling class at the time of its initiation. The rural reform program has been steadily gathering momentum; yet it has become very difficult for the government to control the direction it is beginning to take. Unseen divisions are taking place within the peasant class; certain peasants have immensely benefited, while others have suffered declines in real income from the changes initiated after 1963.[7] As an example, the administration of the reform has been weak, and implementation is inadequate in most areas because of the lack of managers, agricultural engineers, and agronomists. A vital element in the reform—cooperatives—exists largely on paper, and those that are operating lack skilled supervisors and managers.[8] Different forms of farm cooperatives have been introduced on an experimental basis, but in most cases their performance has been dismal.[9]

Meanwhile the villagers, frustrated by broken promises and new expectations, have been increasing their demands for reform. The government's literacy program has led to demands for further education and the right to attend secondary and vocational schools. The scattered but nationwide coverage of the Health Corps (one group set up to implement the White Revolution) has led many villagers without these services to appeal for doctors, clinics, and hospitals. Many rural villagers who were told by the Shah that they were to begin new lives now see themselves as victims of government agents.

But even where the reform programs have met with moderate success, new problems have arisen. Younger villagers, by means of literacy and land reforms, are beginning to acquire the tools that will enable them to penetrate the middle class in increasing numbers. One of the major unintended consequences of the White Revolution is the accelerating growth of the professional middle class. Yet this is the same class that is becoming more alienated and thus threatens the traditional socioeconomic system. At the same time, this class is needed to control and guide the explosive land reform programs.

In terms of numbers, the professional middle class increased by over 60 percent between 1956 and 1966. By the mid-1960s over half a million employed Iranians were part of that class. With the acceleration of reform programs and the continued growth of the educational system, there is every indication that this class will continue to burgeon and develop rapidly. Although it still represents a relatively small percentage of the total Iranian population, its relative increase has been great. In 1956 approximately one out of every seventeen Iranians belonged to the professional middle class.[10] Ten years later the proportion had become one in twelve.

The Shah's Dilemma

The optimal method of allocating its oil revenues is the crux of the development planning problem in Iran. In the past, the results obtained by the government's expenditures were unsatisfactory because the planners were not able to predict the manner in which those expenditures would aid in the country's development. A more serious deficiency arising from the expenditures has been that they have often caused a number of adverse effects, effects which will take a long time to rectify.

As a result, a major rethinking of the country's development strategy seems to be taking place. This reevaluation has been compelled by a single fact: the unparalleled economic growth rates of the 1960s, but particularly the rapid acceleration in GNP in the early to middle 1970s, has had little or no effect on most of the country's poeple, who continue to live in desperate poverty. Contrary to government expectations, output increases in industries and projects financed by the oil revenues have failed to "trickle down" to the poorer half or even two-thirds of the population. Those most favored by the country's growth—the industrialists (particularly those receiving high tariffs), civil servants, and skilled industrial workers—have generally been able to absorb all the increases in GNP. This basic weakness in the country's development process—the inability to spend oil revenues in a manner that benefits the general population—is the principal source of social turmoil. Unrest, particularly in the rural areas, has been latent for some time, but it is now surfacing in the form of peasant protests, student demonstrations, and increased terrorist activities.

A dilemma now faces the Iranian political elite. First, the elite must enlist the participation and commitment of one of the very classes that threatens them in order to implement and control the Shah's reforms. Second, many of those peasants who benefit from the reforms will move into the already expanding professional middle class, and here they will form another source of threat to the existing status quo. Whether a Marxian type of revolution develops obviously depends on the way the government is able to control the economy for the betterment of the people. If the officials are obsolete[11] in Marxian terms, that is, if they cannot utilize the oil revenues effectively for the development of the whole economy, then they will become more and more vulnerable to those groups who are now in a position, because of their educational and technical superiority, to achieve better results and who are alienated because they feel that the incompetence of their leaders is reducing their chances of ever fulfilling their cultural and economic potentials.

By now it has become clear that if the Iranian economy continues to move in its current direction, if the oil revenues fall off, and if the structural maladjustments in the economy mount, the system undoubtedly will, as Marx described, collapse. The ultimate breakdown will be occasioned by the very large increases in the disparities of income and wealth which the country's high economic growth rates have facilitated.

A Hegelian Analysis of Change

The above analysis is one that a Marxist would probably derive through use of the dialectic. Yet there is nothing inherent in the Hegilian dialectic that would inescapably lead to the Marxian conclusions. Marx, in fact, differs from Hegel in two important respects. First, his theory of history is based on a single element—the productive process, that is, the change in technology (always labor-saving). Marx selected technology as the sole independent variable in describing a nation's economic growth and associated sociopolitical trends. According to Marx, the mode of production causes everything to follow a deterministic pattern in a society, since the dialectic operates over time. There is nothing in the Hegelian system, however, that selects a single element with such special power or independence; that is, a number of elements interact in his system, none of which is necessarily dominant over the others.

Second, Hegel did not intend to treat the dialectic as a predictive instrument; he notes that any philosophy is developed too late after events have occurred to teach the world what it should be—"the owl of Minerva," according to Hegel, "begins its flight when the shades of twilight have already fallen."[12]

The approach taken here is to utilize a bit of both philosophers' contributions in making a more realistic long-run forecast for the economy than the surprise-free simulations. In structuring this approach, we first discard the Marxian contention that socioeconomic systems are deterministic and in particular that capitalism (or at least the Iranian version of it) will contradict itself out of existence and suffer a violent overthrow. Second, we accept Marx's use of the Hegelian dialectic as a powerful tool for forecasting.

Conclusions

Our approach to forecasting is sympathetic with the Marxist notion of change: (1) As Marxists contend, theory which does not end in action is sterile, and action without the supporting theory is without meaning or purpose. (2) As Marxists contend, any statement, pronouncement, or promise by an individual or political party cannot be taken at face value. An idea or theory is proved correct or incorrect, true or false, by how it works out in practice and by the changes it brings about. What someone thinks or believes and says, or the motivation behind it, at any given moment, is quite another matter. (3) As Marxists contend, the object of theory or philosophy (Hegel notwithstanding) is not merely to understand the world but to change it, since understanding and change are organically linked.

Marxists often say "man does what he must," or more formally, "man is truly free only when he does that which is historically necessary." Our forecast can be called Hegelian rather than Marxian, since we are looking at Iran's problem more from the point of view of the state. It is Hegelian, therefore, in that it says the "state must do what it must."[13] It must undertake certain actions to survive in its current form.

Notes

1. As reported in the *Kayhan* (Weekly International Edition), May 3, 1975, p. 4.

2. In a lesser known work, *The White Revolution*, the Shah makes many of these same points. Cf. Mohammed Rexa Shah Pahlavi, *The White Revolution* (Tehran: Imperial Pahlavi Library, 1967). It should be noted that the Shah's books are "ghostwritten," yet reflect quite accurately his views.

3. Mohammed Reza Shah Pahlavi, *Mission for My Country* (London: Hutchinson, 1961), p. 85.

4. An excellent interpretation of Marx's views of the European revolutions is given in John Sanderson, *An Interpretation of the Political Ideas of Marx and Engels* (London: Longmans, 1969).

5. The word "obsolesence" has a number of interpretations in Marxian literature. Here we interpret it to be the lag of institutions (and their leaders) behind technology; that is, the very existence of prevailing institutions, ideas, codes, etc., of a set character introduces a time lag between a change in the economic base and corresponding changes in the superstructure (religion, moral codes, political beliefs, etc.). Marxian

theory, as interpreted here, maintains that a given change in the productive force is followed by a period (of undefined length) during which there occurs a gradual, imperceptible change in production relations and the various elements of the ruling class. The new will eventually and inevitably win out over the old, according to Marxists, but not without a struggle. Cf. Alexander Balinky, *Marx's Economics* (Lexington, Mass.: D.C. Heath, Lexington Books, 1970), chapter 3.

6. One of the most vocal has been Bahman Nirumand (living in Germany). See his *Iran: The New Imperialism in Action* (New York: Monthly Review Press, 1969).

7. Cf. S. Thomas Stickley and Bahaoldin Najafi, "The Effectiveness of Farm Corporations in Iran," *Tahqiqat-e Eqtesadi*, Winter 1971, for a survey of the income distribution patterns caused by the land reforms.

8. Kenneth Blatt, *Land Reform in Iran* (Washington: Agency for International Development, 1970), pp. 93–95.

9. An excellent survey of the different types of farm organizations in Iran is given by Abdolhossain Zehedani, "Iran: Evaluation of Agricultural Development Strategy," Unpublished Ph.D. dissertation, University of California (Davis, 1974).

10. Cf. references to Iranian Censuses of 1956 and 1966. It should be noted that the class structure in Iran does contain a number of overlaps, so that while the intelligentsia are usually referred to as "middle class," a few are in the elite and also a number are in the peasant or lower classes. Cf. Marvin Zonis, *The Political Elite of Iran* (Princeton: Princeton University Press, 1971) for a thorough discussion of class distinctions and attitudes.

11. Cf. note 6 above. "Obsolete" would mean in this context that the rulers were not capable of utilizing the new means of production—oil revenues and imported technology—to the best advantage of the country.

12. Frank Tuilly and Ledger Wood, *A History of Philosophy* (New York: Henry Hold and Company, 1958), pp. 480–81.

13. This quote is not ascribed to Hegel. In fact, Hegel's position regarding the theory of the state is still a matter of controversy. For a recent summary of the debate over this area of Hegelian philosophy, cf. Sholomo Avineri, *Hegel's Theory of the Modern State* (Cambridge: Cambridge University Press, 1972).

9

The Hegelian Synthesis

Introduction

The key issue arising from the Iranian economic performance during the last decade is how long economic growth can be sustained without a more concerted effort to solve a number of the country's underlying social and income distribution problems. Economic growth and socioeconomic development in Iran are not necessarily synonymous. Iran's experience leading up to the White Revolution in the early 1960s offers a clear example of growth without development.[1] And with the increase in oil revenues after the overthrow of Dr. Mossadegh, the Iranian economy was able to achieve for a time a high rate of growth associated with little or no social development, intensified unemployment, widened disparities in the income distribution, and the stagnation of educational opportunities. This roughly describes the developments during the 1955–1962 period.

The Shah intended the White Revolution to alter this pattern of development toward one more concerned with social development. But his critics have categorized the White Revolution as a series of preventive or stopgap measures aimed at averting the initiation of real economic and social reforms.[2] The motivating force behind the revolution, according to these writers, was the maintenance of the status quo with a small ruling elite benefiting from the economic gains while the majority of the population reaped little but promises and an occasional handout.[3]

Those who justify the Shah's authoritarian regime do so on the assumption that this form of government is more effective in the Iranian context than a democracy would be in achieving high rates of economic growth. They point to the fact that eventually a more prosperous population will be in a better position to create a permanent democracy.[4] The experiences of the past, not only in Iran but in other developing countries as well, elicit the question of whether even an authoritarian regime can sustain a high rate of economic growth without giving adequate attention to the basic problem of unequal income distribution, low labor productivity, and increasing rural stagnation.

The lesson since the 1973 oil price increases is that in Iran even under the most favorable financial circumstances, economic growth, social progress, and "liberty"—the respect for human rights—do not necessarily advance jointly. In particular, it appears that the economic growth pattern since 1973 has been associated with social and political retrogression. How long this retrogression can continue is a matter of speculation. The surprise-free forecasts based on the existing economic mechanisms in the country indicate that increasing urban-rural income inequalities are associated with higher growth rates. Because these models contained no direct feedback mechanism from the consequences of increasing inequality to other facets of the economy, one can only sepeculate as to the maximum deterioration in income distribution that would have to take place before growth would be halted by civil and political strife. To modify and lend reality to our forecasts, therefore, a Hegelian synthesis of the two plans—the high-growth plan versus the social equality plan—is required.

Whereas the White Revolution was based on the premise that "all good things go together," there is an equally just argument that might result with increasing disparities of income, that is, "all bad things go together." The second eventuality thus is becoming the mirror image of the former.

The Shah's Vision of the Future

The euphoria surrounding Iran's unprecedented increase in oil revenues enabled the Shah to envisage a rising new generation of Iranians who will have every opportunity to lead a full and productive life. His speeches often refer to the period until the end of the century as "a new era in Iran of great civilization." According to the Shah, Iranian society at the end of the century will be one that has eliminated many of the major worries that concern the population today—the lack of financial security, limited availability of adequate educational opportunities, and so on. He hopes to achieve something akin to a utopian dream. He is apparently serious, and his plans are based on the utilization of vast oil revenues.

Great civilization in Iran, as the Shah has begun revealing (beginning with the formation and consolidation of the Rastakhiz Party), is a series of new revolutionary principles—extensions of the White Revolution that will entail resource utilization for the common good in a highly productive, technologically creative industrial society. According to the Shah, the new Iran will treasure every one of its members; it will be concerned with the welfare of all, and will grant to each one a degree of social security unrivaled anywhere in the world.

At least one sympathetic observer, Gregory Lima,[5] believes that the new principles of the White Revolution differ from the earlier ones in that they are more directly concerned with social welfare. According to Lima,[6] the Shah's intention is for the people to relate his new concept of development to their lives and aspirations, absorbing it into their thinking.

Finally, when the Shah thinks the time is right, the concept may be expressed as a basic principle of the revolution.

Even the most sympathetic observers admit that the new Iranian revolution will entail changes that cannot happen overnight. The Shah's strategy, however, is to pursue many interrelated measures simultaneously, one presumably gaining support from and benefiting from the others. The key to successful development through the revolution, according to the Shah's aides, is constant alertness by the Shah, the exercise of leadership qualities, diagnosis of the capabilities and weaknesses of each institution and those factors required to achieve its objectives, and the use of pragmatic solutions to otherwise knotty problems that may take too much time to resolve by classic evolutionary methods.

As Lima[7] concludes, "Thus the process and progress in Iran has virtually no precedent in classical economic and social theory."

The Nonrational Basis of Planning Decisions in Iran

The Shah's goal of guiding the country along a desirable path, though very commendable, seems somewhat beyond his and the nation's capabilities. Despite grandiose talk of the future wealth and economic strength of the country, neither the government nor the Shah has developed a well-defined set of national priorities. The vagueness surrounding the nation's and the Shah's long-run goals has resulted in poor project selection; that is, projects are chosen not for their contribution to a set of long-run objectives, but more often on strictly noneconomic grounds.[8] Many projects are selected on the basis of (1) their "impact," (2) the "vindication principle," and (3) available funds.

"Impact projects" in Iran are quite often large and impressive (in size of design) but very marginal economically. These programs, however, are justified by the Shah on specifically political grounds, and for that reason they have been selected. This was the case with the steel mill at Isfahan and with the industries located in western Iran, where comparisons with the Iraqi development effort are easy to make.

Another irrational element in the Shah's selection of development projects that is inhibiting the achievement of his long-run goals is the "vindication principle"; that is, the choices of many obviously noneconomic projects are vindicated on historical precedents. For example, even though expanded oil revenues permit extensive rural development programs of feeder roads, which enable farmers to become more integrated into the national economy, the inefficient and expensively maintained railroad system is allocated large amounts of money because the Shah's father, Reza Shah, built railroads, and the wisdom of Reza Shah, the "model of modern Iran," must be vindicated.

Finally, Iran's immense oil revenues enable the government to undertake specifically "chosen" problems that have no real urgency to be undertaken. A good example of the "chosen" project or program is the educational reforms undertaken to alleviate illiteracy. The poor quality of the new schools has only led to frustration among students and increased demands for far more vigorous policies—far better schools than the authorities are capable or even willing to provide.

The Shah's view seems to be that the state is endowed with a will (his) of its own, such as the urge to expand its (the state's) power in relation to other states or the desire to achieve high rates of income growth. The state therefore has an interest which it pursues and is capable of achieving singlemindedly. Yet, because of the number of adverse effects that have stemmed from or been directly related to the implementation of chosen problems, a number of pressing problems have developed.

For example, the land reforms that have taken place over the last decade are spawning some unfortunate side effects. The beneficiaries of the reform are a minority of the peasantry, and other rural groups, the landless laborers in particular, may possibly be less well off than before the reform.

A related line of attack on the Shah's social and political reform emphasized that the beneficiaries of reform measures are frequently different from those for whom the measures were originally (or ostensibly) taken and intended. Low-cost housing projects, as social programs intended for the poor and as expenditures on public goods in general, end up benefiting primarily the upper-class contractors and industrialists.

A major cause of failure to achieve better results from government action in Iran, however, stems from the fact that most of the country's problems are not dealt with directly. One should be mindful of Marx's famous dictum that "mankind always takes up only such problems as it can solve" and of Lindblom's elaboration to the effect that "preception of a problem or definition of a goal often follows and is stimulated by the identification of a possible policy."[9] The understanding of a problem and motivation to attack it are two necessary inputs into policy making, but the timing of these two ingredients can be, as is often the case in the United States, out of phase; that is, understanding can pace motivation (as assumed by Marx and Lindblom). The Iranian situation, however, is characterized more by motivation to solve a problem before the problem's nature and possible solution are understood. This limitation often results in the authorities importing "solutions" from the outside, in the form of such planning aids as the most up-to-date central banking legislation, economic planning models, and information systems. The result, of course, is the increasing frustration of the Shah because these institutions are often established by the PBO and other ministries who lack even a minimal understanding of the problems they are set up to resolve.

The motivation-outruns-understanding approach to problem solving has increased with the ability of the country to undertake more expenditures with the increased oil revenues. Planning in Iran under the Shah's impatience for results has exhibited a pattern of rushing in with impulsive pseudosolutions.

The policy-making process so much in evidence in Iran can be categorized by the "issue-attention cycle," which has a number of phases:

1. The "preproblem state" is that during which the existing problem is not recognized by the authorities, largely because it was not anticipated.
2. Then comes the "alarmed discovery and euphoric enthusiasm"; that is, the problem is considered a priori fully solvable "if we can devote sufficient effort (money) to it."
3. In the next phase, it is realized that solving the problem may be too much trouble or costly and in any case probably goes against the immediate interests of the elite or other influential groups.
4. As a result of this realization, the authorities begin a gradual decline in their public statements about the problem. This is helped by the providential appearance of another problem (the Iraquis are massing on the border, for example) that will occupy the limelight.
5. Finally, there is the "postproblem state," which differs from the preproblem state in that a number of efforts and agencies that have been set up to solve the problem continue to exist and may actually make some quiet progress. Moreover, once the problem has passed through the cycle, it will continue to receive a modicum of public attention.

The Shah, for the reasons discussed above, is in fact the ruler of a coping state rather than one that fits his view of the state as a maker of the future. The idea of the coping state[10] does not have as bad a connotation as might appear at first sight if it is recognized that coping takes place within constraints arising out of the maintenance needs of the basic social and political structure of the country. These constraints, however, are least visible when, as in the case of Iran, the existing social and political structures and institutions are wholly unchallenged. An interesting paradox is beginning to develop in Iran: It is precisely the period of the early 1970s when, because of political consolidations and massive oil revenues, the state is at its strongest that its leaders appear to be just coping, that is, forever handling the matters that somehow require immediate attention without pursuing any grand design. In other words, the more firmly established the power of the Shah, the more he and his aides give the impression of not having formulated any grand design for the future but instead seem to spend most of their time just "putting out fires." Perhaps it is by virtue of this paradox that the phrase "muddling through" is coming to categorize decision making in Iran.

On the other hand, when control weakens, as was the case when the oil revenues fell off in the late 1950s and the existing social and political structures were under serious attack, the state is challenged to adapt the old order to new circumstances and is more likely to undertake autonomous policy making. Again such action is likely to only lead to a host of new problems.

Instead of accepting planning as a matter of routine and hence approaching each new problem as it arises with measured forethought, the planners in Iran usually act only on the specifics of a plan when pressured and only then in a state of near panic. It is not surprising that so many planning efforts in Iran have ended in failure.

A final set of problems inhibiting the Shah's ability to achieve his long-run vision for the country are those that arise from within his government rather than from without. He must choose between competing candidates for official positions, adjudicate conflicts between government agencies and between groups comprising himself and his aides, and deal with demands for public spending on all kinds of government-generated projects. The relation between outside and inside pressures is complex in Iran. On the one hand, outside pressures are translated into and exacerbate inside pressures, as when, for example, a worsening income distribution leads to conflicting advice as to the best way to restore equity. On the other hand, when outside pressures decline as a result of the increasing authoritarian stand the government is currently taking, the meetings and other channels through which citizens can voice their protests are prohibited. Under these circumstances, conflict and intrigue within government often increase sufficiently to keep the aggregate pressure on the Shah at a high peak. The result is the spectacle of an authoritarian government that must cope with the pressures arising from its own ranks which leaves it little time for the construction of a grand design for the country.

A major reason, therefore, for the authorities' failure to utilize their vast oil revenues more fully for the betterment of the economy is that no constructive discussions along Hegelian lines are taking place between the Shah and the people. Because of the absence of dialogue of this sort, it is increasingly difficult for the Shah to achieve his vision of what Iran should be by the end of the century.

Economic Growth: Income Distribution Conflicts

The ability of the Shah and his advisers to solve the country's income distribution (social equity) problems through more rational socioeconomic planning will largely determine the pattern of development the country assumes for the remaining quarter of a century. They will need to study the income distribution problem within a comprehensive planning framework, since the income distribution process is a phenomenon originating in economic, social, and political causes. The study and analysis of its causes overflow the bounds of strict economics and will require the interdisciplinary work of economists, mathematicians, statisticians, sociologists, historians, and philosophers. The usual theories that have been resorted to for insights into the problem, that is, the orthodox (pre-Keynesian) and neo-orthodox (Keynesian and post-Keynesian) theories of income distribution, can explain only certain secondary causes of income distribution patterns.[11] What is lacking in Iran is a complete explanation of why, when, and how the country's existing income dis-

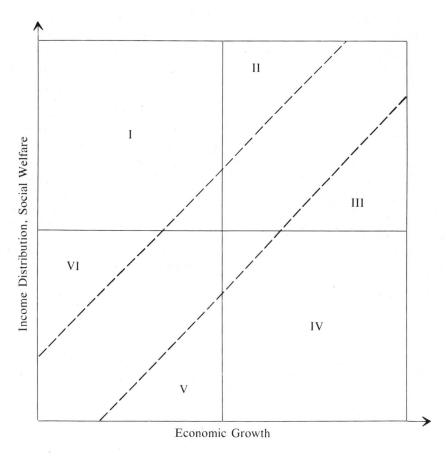

Fig. 9–1. Income Distribution–Economic Growth Matrix.

tribution was established, what the economic, political, and social consequences of this distribution will be, and how new patterns of income distribution (presumably more equitable) can be established.

Hegelian dialectic as applied to the long-run growth of the Iranian economy is intended to shed light on the pattern of income distribution and the limits within which income distribution can fluctuate without upsetting the nation's fragile balance between economic growth and social welfare.

The relationship between economic growth and income distribution can be depicted within the Hegelian framework as: economic growth $\longleftrightarrow$ income distribution.

The double-headed arrow indicates that economic growth in Iran can contribute to improvements in income distribution,[12] and vice versa.

The greater the disparity between rates of GNP growth and a measure of income distribution, such as urban-rural per capita consumption levels, the greater the class tensions. As Marx indicated, it is impossible to analyze income distribution as a strictly economic phenomenon without running into the grave risk of falling into abstractions far removed from reality (obviously a very dangerous basis upon which to formulate an economic policy).

In this context, one of the chief contributions of the Marxian literature is the concept of the risk of revolution. No measurement of this risk is ever given by Marxists; however, in practice, increasing rates of unemployment, concentration of wealth, and a progressive deterioration in the income distribution all form the basis of class struggle and revolution. (Unstable situations in the Marxian sense are shown in Figure 9–1 as areas above and below the dotted region. The corresponding implications for Iran in terms of a likely set of socioeconomic situations are given in Table 9–1.)

Hegelian Methodology

Today hardly any economic or philosophical school of thought would deny the usefulness of dialectical concepts in problem solving. But opinions as to their relevance and applicability in expanding our economic knowledge (and, of course, knowledge in general) vary considerably.

At one extreme we find the Chicago school of thought,[13] proclaiming that whatever the purpose and uses of dialectical concepts, these concepts are antagonistic to the advancement of economic science: knowledge proper exists only to the extent to which it is expressed in mathematical concepts, or at a minimum deductive logic—not dialectical logic. Their proposition recalls that of the Catholic Church: holy thought can be expressed only in Latin.

Table 9-1
Matrix of Economic Growth-Income Distribution Combinations in Iran

	Economic Growth	Economic Decline
Equitably Distributed Income	A solid base for a stable political economic and social situation. Economic development sustained and stimulated by a high growth rate of the gross national product.	Precarious and even fictitious social welfare. Fertile ground for increasing inequalities in income distribution and for modifications in established power relationships through revolution. Workers, rural educated, and intelligentsia politically active.
Unequitably Distributed Income	Precarious stability. Frequent social conflict. Income and wealth highly concentrated. Monopolies dominate economic political activity.	Economic, politcal, and social instability. Regressive income distribution becomes worse with time. Land and wealth ownership highly concentrated. Apparent stability of monarchy eroding owing to increasing illiteracy.

Source: Compiled by author.

At the other end of the methodological spectrum there are the Hegelians of all strains maintaining that knowledge is attained only with the aid of dialectical notions in the strict Hegelian sense, that is, notions to which the principle "A is non-A" applies always.

There is a definite asymmetry between the two opposing schools of logic—one using mathematics or mathematical symbols and the other shunning them as tools. However no Hegelian—Hegel included—has ever denied the tremendous additional power that the dialectic can possess if it is built around a mathematical formulation. The main advantage of a mathematical formulation is that it posseesses a built-in device against most kinds of errors of thought that dialectical concepts in nonmathematical form do not have. Because of the predominance of the nonmathematical use of the dialectic, we are apt to associate dialectical concepts with "fuzzy" or at best loose thinking. The famous expression "the muddied waters of Hegelian dialectics" speaks for itself.

An Operational Hegelian System

One advantage of the Hegelian type of analysis, as developed here, as an aid to making a realistic long-run forecast of the Iranian economy is that it is capable of examining a complex and interrelated problem, such as income distribution and growth, in mathematical form and of using data of uncertain quality. The Hegelian model can identify variables controllable by the government and determine the probability that the government will have to use these tools to have the desired impact on the economic goals sought. Both problems of uncertainty are dealt with by combining the Hegelian dialectic with a powerful mathematical decision tool—Markov chains.[14] Within the Hegelian-Markov framework it is assumed that the nation's decision makers (the Shah, PBO, and the Economic Council) are willing to engage in a constructive dialogue with other segments of the economy, such as the intelligentsia and rural groups. The outcome of this dialectic debate is the assignment of probabilistic values to the likelihood that the authorities will undertake certain actions to achieve an urban-rural income distribution pattern that is less unequal than those indicated as likely by the surprise-free forecast. Use of this approach assumes the macroeconomic models such as those in Appendix B, so that the planners can anticpate the impact of the policy tools at their disposal.

For purposes of illustrating the Hegelian dialectic, we have taken simulation 3 from the surprise-free forecast. This forecast can be assumed to be the government's plan for high growth; equity considerations are given a secondary role. As noted (Table 6–5), this simulation gives an overall average rate of growth of 12.71 for the period until the end of the century. During that time, however, the urban-rural per capita income ratio (our measure of inequality in the income distribution) increases from 2.129 in 1972 to 2.865 in 1980, reaching a maximum of 5.189 in 1997, then falling to 5.146 in 2000. High rates of growth (real growth in constant prices) therefore may, if uncontrolled, result in greatly increased income disparities in Iran.

With initiation of the White Revolution, the Shah appears to be attempting to pull the country into a stable situation (indicated by the dotted lines between quadrants II and I in Figure 9–1). But his attempts have not been altogether successful. (If anything, the country is moving further toward the bottom left-hand corner of quadrant VI.)

The crux of Iran's development problem, therefore, is how to control growth and income distribution in a manner that yields stability (that is, a path from quadrant VI into the range between II and I).

This is accomplished within our framework by assuming that the decision makers in Iran are willing, after the structured dialectic debate, to assign values to a set of well-defined objectives, and that the PBO is then able to specify outcomes of programs that can be directly related to these objectives (that grow within the stability range of Figure 9–1). For illustration we have assumed that the compromise solution is one in which the economy must still grow at high rates, yet the differential between urban and rural incomes cannot increase above 3.0. Also there must be an improvement in equity and social welfare by the end of the century. This is shown by requiring the urban-rural per capita income differential to drop to 1.3 by the year 2000. There are at least two major policy variables for accomplishing these objectives—government investment and private investment; that is, given the current conditions in Iran, a 1-rial increase in government investment increases urban consumption by 0.47 rial; a 1-rial increase in private investment increases rural consumption by 0.13 rial (Appendix B). Thus by controlling both expenditures—lowering government expenditure and raising private investment (perhaps through changes in fiscal policy—transfers, tax changes, and so on)—it is possible for the authorities to control the distribution of income over time.

Operationally Hegelian-Markovian examination of the economy begins with a sensitivity analysis in which a set of private and government investment expenditures is selected. These expenditures in turn determine a series of income distribution patterns. Each alternative pattern is then examined to ascertain if it is possible to change the pattern of expenditures and obtain a higher "payoff," that is, more private consumption without loss of the 12.71 growth rate. The optimal pattern of government and private investment is then determined through an iterative process, giving finally that combination of expenditures that yields the largest "payoff."

For the Markovian resource allocation model used here, a set of stringent constraints on income distribution was always operative. The results indicate that the country in the surprise-free forecast is trying to grow too fast too soon;[15] that is, in achieving its overall average annual rate of investment of 15.54 for the 1972–2000 period, government investment grows rapidly at first (20.59 per annum) between 1972 and 1976, then decelerates over time (18.26 for 1976–1982; 16.35 for 1980–1985; 14.79 for 1985–1990; 13.26 for 1990–1995; and 11.74 for 1995–2000).

Since government investment has its greatest impact on urban consumption, it is possible to achieve the same level of total investment over the period by gradually accelerating its rate of increase. The result is to maintain aggregate GNP growth and the income distribution goals. In graphical terms, the restructuring of private and government expenditures moves the economy into a optimal state of growth and equality, (the dotted region of Figure 9–1) and then allows the economy to expand within this distribution pattern.

Conclusions

The Hegelian-Markovian analysis of the Iranian economy indicates why the economy is currently in trouble: it is trying to grow too fast, thus necessitating the current borrowing in international capital markets. The country is not short of resources, but it must control its allocations over time in a manner that is amenable to achieving certain clear-cut objectives—in this case, growth with equality. The pattern of growth generated by the model indicates that the country could actually run a large surplus for investment overseas if it reduced government investment rates for the next decade. From that time on it would be able to reap the returns from this investment if oil revenues declined.

It is clear that there is room for improvement in policy making in Iran. As a step toward utilizing the nation's resources more effectively, the country must develop macroeconomic models capable of:

1. Employing the essence of the policy-making process, that is, providing a mechanism for estimating the appropriate tradeoff between conflicting goals
2. Recognizing the uncertain nature of the country's political process (that is, the policy maker's tradeoffs or the relative weights associated with each objective are often not known with certainty)
3. Using techniques sufficiently general so that they are useful to the planners and the decision makers (they should rely on a minimum number of assumptions)
4. Converging to alternative solutions that would most likely be accepted by the major segments of the population

We believe the Hegelian-Markovian approach outlined meets these requirements and hence is an initial step toward a realistic forecast of the growth of Iran to 2000 A.D.

Notes

1. For a striking similarity in another context, cf. Robert W. Clower et al., *Growth Without Development* (Evanston, Ill.: Northwestern University Press, 1966). Clower observes that Liberia was a prime example of both an enclave and a dual economy. Despite its rich resource base—rubber and iron—few advances were made in transforming the subsistence sector of the economy, nor was there (1966) any prospect of significant progress. The economic backwardness of Liberia was, according to Clower, not attributable either to lack of resources or to domination of foreign financial and political interests. Rather, the underlying difficulty was that the traditional leaders of Liberia had not permitted those changes necessary to develop the society and its economy. Clower et al., p. 4.

2. George Baldwin has noted that land reform, like so many reforms in Iran, cannot be assessed except in terms of Iranian political behavior. Seen from this perspective (Baldwin was in Iran at the time), no Iranian land reform is likely to achieve its aims until there have first been much more fundamental changes in the political system than have yet occurred. Cf. George Baldwin, *Planning and Development in Iran* (Baltimore: Johns Hopkins Press, 1967), p. 98.

3. Bahman Nirumand, *Iran: The New Imperialism in Action* (New York: Monthly Review Press, 1969) continually stresses this point.

4. Cf. Gregory Lima et al., *The Revolutionizing of Iran* (Tehran: International Communicators Iran, 1973), chapter 2.

5. Gregory Lima, "Towards an Ideal Society," *Kayhan* (International Edition), January 31, 1976, p. 4.

6. *Ibid.*

7. *Ibid.*

8. The elements of nonrationality in development planning in Iran have been excellently described by Norman Jacobs, *The Sociology of Development, Iran as a Case Study* (New York: Praeger Publishers, 1966), chapter 3. See his *Modernization Without Development: Thailand as an Asian Case Study* (New York: Praeger Publishers, 1971) for a similar planning situation in quite another environment.

9. Cf. Charles Lindblom, "The Science of 'Muddling Through,' " *Public Administration Review* 79–88, 1959.

10. The situation in governmental decision making in Iran (because of the rather closed power structure) can in large part be examined in terms of problem solving within large firms. It can be argued that officials in Iran as members of companies in the United States make satisfactory rather than optimal choices in problem-solving and decision-making situations. Furthermore, these problem-solving behavior routines are based on past experience, rules of thumb, etc. Within organizations, a member will aspire to achieve two sets of goals, personal and organizational, and it is not necessary for the two sets of goals to be internally consistent. These ideas have been extended to the concept of organizations as being continually in a latent state of conflict regarding resource allocations. Quasi-resolution of the conflict is achieved through internal bargaining about goals or their redefinition and about the means to achieve these goals. For the theory as applied to United States firms, cf. R. M. Cery and J. G. March, *A Behavioral Theory of the Firm* (Englewood Cliffs, N.J.: Prentice-Hall, 1963); and J. G. March and H. A. Simon, *Organizations* (New York: John Wiley & Sons, 1958).

11. Cf. Hollis Chenery et al., *Redistribution with Growth* (Oxford: Oxford University Press, 1974) for a rigorous discussion of the various theories of income distribution. A particularly insightful discussion on the theories of the income distribution process is given by R. Gendarme, "Reflections on the Approaches to the Problems of Distribution in Underdeveloped Countries," in Jean Marchal and Bernard Ducros, eds., *The Distribution of National Income* (London: Macmillan, 1968), chapter 14.

12. Cf. Robert Looney, *The Determinants of Income Distribution in Semi-industrialized Countries: A Case Study of Iran, Mexico, Brazil, and*

South Korea (New York: Praeger Publishers, 1975), chapter 7.

13. The different methodologies used in the examination of the development of countries over time are expertly summarized in T. Y. Shen, "Approaches to Economic Development," *The Malayan Economic Review* 14–27, April 1964. A more recent summary along these lines is given in Richard Day, "Orthodox Economists and Existential Economics," *Journal of Economic Issues,* June 1975. Day makes an important distinction between three basic methodologies. The first is the realm of existing analytical knowledge. The orthodox operate from niches within this realm. He identifies a second realm of *possible* analytical knowledge. Finally, there is the third realm of dialectical knowledge, "so unfamiliar to conventional economists." Day, *ibid.,* p. 235.

14. There is a great degree of flexibility in the construction of Markovian chains. We have developed a Markovian decision model within this general framework. Briefly, to be compatible with the Hegelian dialectic, the system was constructed to be dynamic and to evolve over time according to the joint effect of the probabilistic laws of motion and of the sequence of decisions made by the Iranian authorities. In particular, the economy is assumed to be monitored by the authorities, and in each planning period (in this case each year) a decision is made concerning what action must be undertaken to achieve certain goals in the future—income distribution patterns, etc. In particular, when the economy is in state i and decision $d_i(R) = k$ (where R is a policy action), then the probability that the economy will be in state j at the next observed time period (year) is given by $P_{ij}(k)$. This procedure results in a sequence of observed states X_0, X_1, . . . and a sequence of decisions made, Δ_0, Δ_1, ... This sequence of observed states and of decisions made is called a Markovian decision process. The term "Markovian" is used because of the underlying assumptions made about the probabilistic laws of motion. The process maximizes an objective over time—in this case, a certain pattern of rural-urban per capita consumption levels—through an exhaustive enumeration of a given set of possible policies. Since it is evident that direct enumeration becomes cumbersome when the number of policies is large, we confined the exercise to only two policies—the level of government and private investment. Cf. Chaiho Kim, *Quantitative Analysis for Managerial Decisions* (Reading, Mass.: Addison-Wesley, 1976), chapter 17, for an introduction to the Markovian processes.

15. While it is impossible to say how "fast" the economy should be growing given its resources, it is fairly clear that the current inflation and other structural problems in Iran are a result of too rapid a rate of growth. For a general discussion along therse lines, cf. Janos Kornai, *Rush Versus Harmonic Growth* (Amsterdam: North Holland Publishing Co., 1972).

10 Iran at the End of the Century

Introduction

Our analysis of the Iranian economy indicates that during the remaining quarter-century Iran will almost certainly have the resources to allow her to grow at a rate of at least 10 percent per annum—this rate would result in a doubling of GNP every seven years. To give an idea of orders of magnitude, by the year 2000 Iran will probably have a population about the same as the present-day England and an outlook for a per capita income somewhat higher than current levels in France. However, it is quite likely that the country's limited oil reserves will have reduced the petroleum sector to a minor role in the economy. If, as is likely, oil ceases to be a major contributor to growth, then the country must begin to establish an economic structure that is competitive on international markets, and a social structure with a more equal distribution of income and wealth. Otherwise the eclipse of oil could force the Iranian economy into a period of sustained economic and political chaos. We cannot have an absolute view of the state of the nation at the end of the century—the assumptions underlying the forecast may not be realized. Still, several conclusions stand out and are valid under a wide variety of circumstances that the country may encounter.

Major Recommendations

In view of the above, the conclusions for policy makers are clear:

1. The Iranian government must continue its expenditures for reducing poverty and eradicating economic distress. Since inflation exacerbates the maldistribution of income, for this reason (among others) the government must use noninflationary means in its fight against poverty
2. The government should continue its special efforts to reduce rural poverty and to bring more of the people now excluded into the market (cash) economy

While the export performance of Iran was quite satisfactory during the 1959–1976 period, it had not matured to a point where a comparative advantage was established in the manufacturing areas. To continue the

137

high rate of growth in GNP during the rest of the decade, it is imperative to:

1. Expand manufacturing exports to replace primary products as sources of foreign exchange
2. Create domestic conditions that will make Iran competitive in the international market for manufactured goods
3. Reduce the deficit on the nonoil sector of the current account in the balance of payments to increase creditworthiness (the government can contribute to this end by reorienting its investment policies to shorten the time required for projects financed by oil revenues to become directly or indirectly earners of foreign exchange)
4. Increase the role of private direct investment in expanding exports, with special regard to the fact that manufactured exports tend to be relatively labor-intensive
5. Expand petroleum exports as rapidly as possible

The fifth requirement raises the question of whether investment in extra refining capacity for exports is the best allocation of scarce capital resources, especially in a period of probable falling oil prices. It also involves the choice between conserving natural resources for future use or using them now to the maximum. Iran can expect to have a higher per capita real income a generation hence, when it should be proportionately less dependent on oil revenues than at present. Both of these considerations point to the wisdom of exporting crude oil now for the benefit of this generation of poorer Iranians rather than conserving it for a richer future generation, when relative prices of energetics and petrochemical feedstocks may have been reduced by changes in technology.

The most important aggregate policy conclusions concerning imports are the following:

1. Iran should lessen its dependence on imports over the next several decades. The economy is unlikely to maintain its existing high rates of growth if it continually requires a large import component during more advanced stages of industrialization
2. The composition of imports will change as the country becomes self-sufficient in consumer goods. The next stage of industrialization, however, involves moving into capital and intermediate goods. The government will have to give careful consideration to the degree and length of time these new industries will need to become efficient
3. The country will have to continue importing technology and skills. Since skills will be a bottleneck, the country may have to shift its import composition toward those areas that are forecast as bottlenecks to the economy's development

4. The country's import capacity is and will continue to be heavily dependent on its transport network and should begin immediately to coordinate the various forms of transport necessary to meet its growth and welfare requirements

Two issues for policy makers with regard to the major sectors stand out:

1. Agricultural productivity must be raised. This will require large capital investment, both in material and in human resources. Private investment can play a large role here and should be encouraged
2. In the interest of industrial efficiency (and here agriculture should count as an industry) based on a sound allocation of productive resources, Iran should be linked to world markets by a more flexible commercial system. Now that capital goods industries are to be encouraged and protected, the stimulus of foreign competition should at least be in the offing. This means moving away from the bureaucratic method of direct import controls through licensing toward freer trade

Conclusions

The major trends during the last quarter-century, as identified by the macroeconomic model, indicate the following.

(1) Oil revenues affect the economy both positively and negatively. On the positive side, they are the prime driving force in increasing national income. On the negative side, they are capable of causing high rates of inflation and increases in the disparity of urban and rural incomes (with increased growth).

(2) The problems arising from rapid growth in the labor force are compounded by accelerated economic growth; thus future increases in growth must be controlled and structured with economic policies oriented toward the goal of minimizing income disparities. Since important parameters of different growth rates (from the demand side) appear to be the rate of rural consumption, these policies must therefore include the introduction of new incentives to locate industrial plants and other forms of economic activity outside Tehran, together with the development of more effective rural education programs than now exist. Given that the Shah has recently moved in these directions, his policies are in this respect fully consistent with the country's long-run needs.

(3) The rates of growth of approximately 12 percent in real terms generated by the macroeconomic model (simulation 3 in particular) are the rates that are expected to materialize over the rest of the century.

(4) Modifying this macroeconomic model with the Hegelian-Markovian modifications, it is possible to obtain a pattern of growth for Iran capable of generating a financial surplus over the next decade. This is in marked contrast to the current budget deficit.

(5) Of course, what matters is the real value of Iran's oil income during the coming years and to what economic uses it flows. Since the future is so uncertain and rapid changes can occur within a short time, any long-term forecasts need to be periodically reviewed. One pessimistic prediction—model 4—shows the implications of falling revenues. In these circumstances the revenues used for foreign investment in earlier periods of high oil revenues might ease balance-of-payments problems during the years of declining oil income, but the financial surpluses invested abroad are unlikely to extend significantly the time when Iran will again have to become a borrowing nation.

(6) In order to maintain a steady growth path over the short, medium, and longer term, it is clear that oil revenues must be divided optimally between those funds destined for internal use according to absorptive capacity and those destined for foreign investments. Clearly, it is possible for the government to overspend and lose all the potential advantages that have accrued to it as a result of the 1973 and 1974 oil price increases.

Appendix A: The Treatment of Oil in the Iranian National Income Accounts

The treatment of oil in the Iranian national income accounts has been a matter of controversy in Iran, and an understanding of the conventions that have been adopted by the Bank Markazi[1] in compiling these accounts is essential for comprehending their impact on the Iranian economy and their relationships to the other major macroeconomic aggregates in the national accounts. Obviously, the very high rates of income recorded for Iran in the last several years are a direct result of the acceleration of oil revenues, but they are also a function of the accounting system used in estimating the national accounts. In the estimation of the GNP in current prices, the value added for oil is included at its market value, and thus a 150 percent or so annual rate of growth in that sector will, of course, translate itself directly into a very high current growth rate for the GNP. In estimating the GNP at constant prices, the value added in the oil sector is deflated for the rise in Iran's import price index. Thus, rather than reflect an increase or decrease in the physical output of oil (that is, in terms of barrels or metric tons), the constant price value added for oil reflects both the change in price and the change in production, as well as a deflation procedure proxied by Iran's import price index. The conventions treating oil in the country's national accounting system assume, therefore, that a rise in oil prices deflated by the import price index represents a rise in real resources, in that the supply of foreign exchange at constant prices has been increased.

The variations of nonoil GNP in current and constant (1972) prices for

Table A-1
Variation in Nonoil GNP in Current and Constant 1972 Prices, 1971–1974

Billion Rials	1971	1972	1973	1974
GNP	962.7	1183.1	1763.3	3020.4
(current prices)	(20.6)	(22.9)	(49.0)	(71.3)
Nonoil GNP	782.4	968.7	1200.7	1597.4
(current prices)	(14.1)	(23.8)	(23.9)	(53.0)
GNP	1036.3	1183.1	1587.3	2270.0
(1971 prices)	(10.1)	(14.2)	(34.2)	(43.0)
Nonoil GNP	856.0	968.7	1090.7	1243.3
(1971 prices)	(3.4)	(13.2)	(12.6)	(14.0)

Source: Bank Markazi Iran, *Annual Report and Balance Sheet,* various issues.
Note: Figures in parentheses indicate annual rates of growth.

141

the 1971–1974 period show a much lower rate of growth than that of total GNP (Table A–1). The contrast in the performance of the respective GNPs is, therefore, as expected. Nonoil GNP growth rates in constant prices are usually in the 10–14 percent range, while those in current prices are in the 20–35 percent range. Needless to say, these figures illustrate the lopsidedness introduced into the economy by the oil price rise.

Note

1. The Bank Markazi calculates the value added in oil through the income approach, i.e., the sum of wages and salaries, rentals, interest depreciation charges for movable and immovable properties, net profits of the National Iranian Oil Company, of the Iranian Oil Operating Companies, and of other oil companies, and Iran's share from the Consortium. For a detailed description of the conventions used by the Bank, including the oil sector in the national accounts, see Economic Research Department, *National Income of Iran* (Tehran: Bank Markazi Iran, 1969), pp. 99–100; Bureau of National Accounts, *National Income of Iran 1959–1972* (Tehran: Bank Markazi Iran, 1973), p. 2.

Appendix B: Iran—
Basic Macroeconomic
Relationships

The amounts shown here are in billions of 1960 rials. The "t-test" statistic is given in parenthesis under the coefficients. r^2 is the goodness-of-fit statistic.

1. $C_t^g = -50.5999 + 0.1328M_{t-1} + 0.2520Y_{t-1}$ $r^2 = 0.9944$
$\qquad\qquad\quad (34.9)\qquad\quad (5.4)$

2. $C_t^u = 10.3901 + 0.0841IG_{t-1} + 0.0076Y_{t-1}$ $r^2 = 0.9993$
$\qquad\qquad\quad (31.1)\qquad\qquad (15.6)$

3. $C_t^R = -184.5 + 16.9062P_t^R + 0.33C_{t-1}^R + 0.323I_{t-1}^{PC}$ $r^2 = 0.9954$
$\qquad\qquad\quad (38.7)\qquad\quad (5.2)\qquad\qquad (17.3)$

4. $C_t^P = C_t^u + C_t^R$

5. $C_t^T = C_t^g + C_t^P$

6. $I_t^{PC} = 4.1236 + 0.304M_{t-1} + 0.8928I_{t-1}^{PC}$ $r^2 = 0.9669$
$\qquad\qquad\quad (12.3)\qquad\quad (19.4)$

7. $I_t^{PM} = -3.8171 + 0.0720VAO_{t-1} + 0.4097I_{t-1}^P$ $r^2 = 0.9586$
$\qquad\qquad\qquad (12.4)\qquad\qquad\quad (2.7)$

8. $I_t^P = I_t^{PM} + I_t^{PC}$

9. $I_t^{gm} = -16.5124 + 0.4728I_{t-1}^{gm} + 0.0246Y_{t-1} + 0.3174I_{t-1}^P$
$\qquad\qquad\qquad (59.6)\qquad\qquad (9.8)\qquad\qquad (5.6)$
$\qquad\qquad\qquad\qquad\qquad\qquad\qquad\qquad\qquad\qquad r^2 = 0.9984$

10. $I_t^{gc} = -12.6667 - 0.3133I_{t-1}^{gc} + 0.6801VAO_{t-1} + 0.3035I_{t-1}^P$
$\qquad\qquad\qquad (77.5)\qquad\qquad (8.0)\qquad\qquad\quad (4.7)$
$\qquad\qquad\qquad\qquad\qquad\qquad\qquad\qquad\qquad\qquad r^2 = 0.9990$

11. $I_t^g = I_t^{gm} + I_t^{gc}$

12. $I^T = I_t^g + I^P$

13. $NEP = 0.12Y_{t-1}$

14. $M_t = 2.7627 + 0.986908I_{t-1}^{gm} + 1.0553VAO_{t-1}$ $r^2 = 0.9987$
$\qquad\qquad\qquad (64.3)\qquad\qquad\quad (3.3)$

15. $E_t = E_0$

16. $VAO_t = VAO_t$

17. $P_t^R = P_0^R$

18. $Y_t = C_t^g + C_t^P + I_t^P + I_t^g + E_t - M_t - NFP_t$

where

C_t^g = government consumption in current year
$_{t-1}$ = imports in previous year
Y_{t-1} = GNP in previous year
C_t^R = rural consumption

C_t^u = urban consumption
P_t^R = rural population
C_t^P = private consumption
I_t^{PC} = private investment in construction
I_t^{PM} = private investment in machinery
VAO_t = value added in oil
I_t^{gm} = government investment in machinery
I_t^{gc} = government investment in construction
I_t^T = total investment
C_t^T = total consumption
NFP_t = net factor payments
E_t = exports

Bibliography

Aammeed, Kamal, and Margaret Bennett, "Iran's Future Economy," *The Middle East Journal*, 418–20, 1975.

Ahluwalia, Montek S., "Income Inequality: Some Dimensions of the Problem," in Hollis Chenery et al., *Redistribution with Growth* (London: Oxford University Press, 1974), pp. 3–37.

Amuzegar, Jahangir, "Atypical Backwardness and Investment Criteria," *Economica Internazionale*, August 1960.

——, "Capital Formation and Development Finance," in Ehsan Yar-Shater, ed., *Iran Faces the Seventies* (New York: Praeger Publishers, 1971), pp. 67–68.

——, "Ideology and Economic Growth in the Middle East," *The Middle East Journal*, 1–2, 1975.

——, and M. Ali Fekrat, *Iran: Economic Development under Dualistic Conditions* (Chicago: University of Chicago Press, 1971).

Avineri, Sholomo, *Hegel's Theory of the Modern State* (Cambridge: Cambridge University Press, 1972).

Avramovic, Dragoslav, "Industrialization of Iran: The Records, the Problems and the Prospects," *Tahqiqat-e Eqtesadi*, 1–13, Spring 1970.

Badii, Yousef, "A Development Program for Iran," unpublished Ph.D. dissertation, University of Cincinnati, 1973.

Baldwin, George, *Planning and Development in Iran* (Baltimore: Johns Hopkins Press, 1967), chapters 1 and 2.

Balinky, Alexander, *Marx's Economics* (Lexington, Mass.: D. C. Heath, Lexington Books, 1970), chapter 2.

Bank Markazi Iran, *Annual Report and Balance Sheet,* various issues.

——, *Bulletin,* various issues.

——, *Investors Guide to Iran,* 1969.

——, "Urban Household Budget Survey in Iran" (Tehran: Economic Statistics Department, 1968).

Banks, Robert, *Financing Economic Development, Fiscal Policy for Emerging Countries* (Chicago: University of Chicago Press, 1968).

Bartsch, William, "The Industrial Labor Force of Iran: Problems of Recruitment, Training and Productivity," *The Middle East Journal* 28–29, Winter 1971.

Behnam, J., "Population," in W. B. Fischer, ed., *The Cambridge History of Iran: Volume I—The Land of Iran* (Cambridge: Cambridge University Press, 1968), p. 483.

Bharier, Julian, *Economic Development in Iran, 1900–1970* (New York: Oxford University Press, 1971), chapter 3.

Blatt, Kenneth, *Land Reform in Iran* (Washington: Agency for International Development, 1970).

Blitzer, C. et al., "A Dynamic Model of OPEC Trade and Projection," *Journal of Development Studies,* December 1975.

Borlin, Max, and Robert Looney, *The Battelle Linear Programming Model of the Iranian Economy* (Tehran: The Plan Organization, 1972).

Brill, James, "The Plasticity of Informal Politics: The Case of Iran," *The Middle East Journal,* 131–51, Spring 1973.

———, *The Politics of Iran: Groups, Classes and Modernization* (Columbus, Ohio: Charles Merrill, 1972).

Cery, R. M., and J. G. March, *A Behavioral Theory of the Firm* (Englewood Cliffs, N.J.: Prentice-Hall, 1963).

Chenery, Hollis et al., *Redistribution with Growth* (Oxford: Oxford University Press, 1974).

Clark, Peter, *Planning Import Substitution* (Amsterdam: North-Holland Publishing Company, 1970).

Clower, Robert W. et al., *Growth without Development* (Evanston, Ill.: Northwestern University Press, 1966).

Day, Richard, "Orthodox Economists and Existential Economics," *Journal of Economic Issues,* June 1975.

Decker, Robert, "Future Economic Developments: A Delphi Survey," *Futures,* 142, April 1974.

Encyclopaedia Britannica, *Great Works of the Western World, Hegel* (Chicago: Encyclopaedia Britannica, 1952).

Ettehad, Mehrad, *An Approach to Government Budgeting in Iran* (New York: United Nations, 1974).

Fesharaki, Fereidun, *Development of the Iranian Oil Industry* (New York: Praeger Publishers, 1976).

Fischer, D. et al., "The Prospects for OPEC: A Critical Survey of Models of the World Oil Market," *Journal of Development Studies,* December 1975.

Galbraith, J. K., *The New Industrial State* (Boston: Houghton Mifflin, 1967).

Gendarme, R., "Reflections on the Approaches to the Problems of Distribution in Underdeveloped Countries," in Jean Marchal and Bernard Ducros, eds., *The Distribution of National Income* (London: Macmillan, 1968), chapter 14.

Georgescu-Roegen, Nicholas, "Economic Growth and Its Representation by Models," *Atlantic Economic Journal* **4:** 1–8, 1976.

Halmon, B. A., "Economic Incentives in OPEC Oil Pricing Policy," *Journal of Development Studies,* December 1975.

Hegel, Georg Wilhem, *The Philosophy of History* (New York: John Wiley & Sons, 1944).

Helmer, Olaf, "An Agenda for Future Research," *Futures* **6:** 3–14 (1975).

Hirschman, A. O., "Obstacles to Development: A Classification and a Quasi Vanishing Act," *Economic Development and Cultural Change,* 385–89, July 1965.

———, "On Hegel, Imperialism, and Structural Stagnation," *Journal of Development Economics* **3:** 1–8, 1976.

International Labor Organization, *Employment and Income Policies in Iran* (Geneva, 1973), chapter 3.

Iranian Statistical Center, *Past Population Trends and Future Forecast of Iran Population up to 1991* (Tehran, 1971), mimeo.

Iran Trade and Industry Publication, *The Fifth Plan, Tehran: An Echo,* Supplement No. 200, March 1973, pp. 3–4.

Isphani, Ahmed Saboonchi, "The Optimization of Economic Resources for Economic Growth in Iran," unpublished Ph.D. dissertation, University of Southern California, 1966.

Jacobs, Norman, *Modernization without Development: Thailand as an Asian Case Study* (New York: Praeger Publishers, 1971).

———, *The Sociology of Development: Iran as a Case Study* (New York: Praeger Publishers, 1966).

Kahn, Herman, and Anthony Weiner, *The Year 2000: A Framework for Speculation on the Next Thirty-Three Years* (New York: Macmillan, 1967).

Kaldor, Nicholas, "A Model of Economic Growth," *Economic Journal,* December 1957.

———, *Strategic Factors in Economic Development* (Ithaca, N.Y.: Cornell University Press, 1967), chapter 1.

Kayhan International, May 3, 1975, pp. 1, 4.

Kheradjou, Abolghasem, "Banking Structure," *Euromoney,* May 1975.

Kim, Chaiho, *Quantitative Analysis for Managerial Decisions* (Reading, Mass.: Addison-Wesley, 1976), chapter 17.

Klein, Laurance, and Jere Behrman, "Econometric Growth Models for the Developing Economy," in L. Klein, ed., *Essays in Honour of Sir Roy Harrod* (London: Oxford University Press, 1971), pp. 167–87.

Kornai, Janos, *Anti-Equilibrium* (Amsterdam: North-Holland Publishing Co., 1971).

————, *Rush Versus Harmonic Growth* (Amsterdam: North-Holland Publishing Co., 1972).

Lewis, Arthur, *Development Planning: The Essentials of Economic Policy* (New York: Harper & Row, 1966).

Lima, Gregory, "Towards an Ideal Society," *Kayhan* (International Edition), January 31, 1976, p. 4.

———— et al., *The Revolutionizing of Iran* (Tehran: International Communicators Iran, 1973), chapter 2.

Lindbeck, Assar, "The Changing Role of the National State," *Kyklos,* **28:** 23–45, 1975.

Linstone, Harold, and Murray Turoff, eds., *The Delphi Method: Techniques and Applications* (Reading, Mass.: Addison-Wesley, 1975).

Looney, Robert E., *The Determinants of Income Distribution in Semi-industrialized Countries: A Case Study of Iran, Mexico, Brazil, and South Korea* (New York: Praeger Publishers, 1975), chapter 7.

————, "Industrial Decentralization in Iran," *University of Santa Clara Business Review,* 1974.

————, "Iran: The Rise of a World Power," *Countermeasures,* May 1975.

MacIntyre, Alasdir, ed., *Hegel: A Collection of Critical Essays* (Garden City, N.Y.: Doubleday & Co., 1972).

March, J. G., and H. A. Simon, *Organizations* (New York: John Wiley & Sons, 1958).

Marcus, Lyn, *Dialectical Economics* (Lexington, Mass.: D.C. Heath, 1975).

Meade, James, "Is the New Industrial State Inevitable?" *Journal of Political Economy,* June 1968.

Ministry of Health, Family Planning Unit, *Projection of Iran's Population* (Tehran, 1968).

Ministry of Interior, *The First Census of Iran* (Tehran, Nov. 1966).

Moore, Richard et al., "Population and Family Planning in Iran," *The Middle East Journal,* 396–408, Autumn 1974.

Morgenstern, Oskar, Klaus Knorr, and Klaus Heiss, *Long Term Projections of Power: Political, Economic, and Military Forecasting* (Cambridge, Mass.: Ballinger Publishing Company, 1973), Part II.

Naraghi, E., "Regional Studies in Iran," in *Multidisciplinary Aspects of Regional Development* (Paris: OECD, 1969).

New York Times, "Iran Said to Put Stress on Barter," August 12, 1976, p. 11.

Nirumand, Bahman, *Iran: The New Imperialism in Action* (New York: Monthly Review Press, 1969).

Oil and Gas Journal, various issues.

Oleson, P. Bjorn, and P. Norregaard Rasmussen, "An Attempt at Planning in a Traditional State: Iran," in Everett E. Haten, ed., *Planning Economic Development* (Homewood, Ill.: Richard D. Irwin, Inc., 1963), pp. 223–24.

Oshima, Harry, "Income Distribution," working paper for the International Labor Organization (Tehran, 1972), mimeo.

Pahlavi, Mohammed Reza Shah, *Mission for My Country* (London: Hutchinson, 1961).

——, *The White Revolution* (Tehran: Imperial Pahlavi Library, 1967).

Pawelson, John, *Latin America: Today's Economic and Social Revolution* (New York: McGraw-Hill, 1964), chapter 10.

Plan and Budget Organization, Planning Division, Planometrics Bureau, *A Twenty Year Macro-Economic Perspective for Iran, 1351–1371* (Tehran, May 1974), mimeo.

——, *Iran's Fifth Development Plan 1973–1978, Revised, A Summary* (Tehran, May 1975).

——, Population and Manpower Bureau, *Iran's Population—Past, Present and Future* (Tehran, 1973).

Plan Organization, Division of Economic Affairs, *The Third Plan Frame, 1341–1346* (Tehran, 1961).

——, National Statistical Center, *National Census of Population and Housing* (Tehran, March 1968).

——, *Report on the Operation of the Second Seven-Year Plan* (Tehran, 1964), Appendix 5.

——, *Fourth National Development Plan, 1968–1972* (Tehran, 1968).

Poullain, Ludwig, "The Major Borrowers on the International Capital Markets This Year," *Euromoney,* 3–6, February 1976.

Pyatt, Graham et al., *Employment and Income Policies for Iran, Mission Working Paper No. 12, Methodology for Macroeconomic Projections* (Geneva: International Labor Organization, 1973), mimeo.

Rischer, Gunter, "The Stock Exchange," *Euromoney,* May 1975.

Samii, Medhi, "Banking Growth," *Euromoney,* May 1975.

Sanderson, John, *An Interpretation of the Political Ideas of Marx and Engels* (London: Longmans, 1969).

Sharpe, Myron, *John Kenneth Galbraith and the Lower Economics* (White Plains, N.Y.: International Arts and Sciences Press, Inc., 1972).

Shen, T. Y., "Approaches to Economic Development," *The Malayan Economic Review*, 14–27, April 1964.

Shoja, Reza Doroudian, "Econometric Models for the Fourth Plan," *Tahqiqat-e Eqtesadi*, **10**: 432–51, 1968.

Solow, Robert, and J. K. Galbraith, "The New Industrial State: A Discussion," *Public Interest*, Fall 1967.

Stockley, Thomas, and Bahaoldin Najafi, "The Effectiveness of Farm Corporations in Iran," *Tahqiqat-e Eqtesadi*, Winter 1971.

Timbergen, J., *On the Theory of Economic Policy* (Amsterdam: North-Holland Publishing Company, 1952).

Tuilly, Frank, and Ledger Wood, *A History of Philosophy* (New York: Henry Hold and Company, 1958), pp. 480–81.

United Nations Economic Commission for Asia and the Far East, *Interregional Trade Projections, Effective Protection and Income Distribution—Volume II Effective Protection* (Bangkok), pp. 62, 69.

Vagar, Nasrollah, "Economic Development in Iran and the Financing of the Gap in the Third Plan," *Middle Eastern Economic Papers*, 1964.

Vakil, Firouz, "An Econometric Model for Iran," *Bulletin*, **11** (Tehran: Bank Markazi Iran, 1972), pp. 115–20.

———, "An Econometric Model for Iran: Estimated Structural Equations," *Bulletin*, **12** (Tehran: Bank Markazi Iran, 1973), pp. 633–55.

———, *Determining Iran's Financial Surplus 1352–1371—Some Management Concepts* (Tehran: Institute for International Political and Economic Papers, 1975).

Waterson, Albert, *Development Planning: Lessons of Experience* (Baltimore: Johns Hopkins Press, 1965), p. 111.

Wilber, Donald N., *Reza Shah Pahlavi: The Resurrection and Reconstruction of Iran* (Hicksville, N.Y.: Exposition Press, 1975).

Zehedani, Abdolhossain, *Iran: Evaluation of Agricultural Development Strategy*, unpublished Ph.D. dissertation, University of California at Davis, 1974.

Zonia, Marvin, *The Political Elite of Iran* (Princeton, N.J.: Princeton University Press, 1971).

Index

About the Author

Robert E. Looney is assistant professor of economics at the University of Santa Clara. He has been faculty member of the University of California at Davis, development economist at the Stanford Research Institute, and senior economist for Louis Berger International. Dr. Looney has served as economic adviser to the governments of Iran, Panama, and Mexico. He earned the B.S. and Ph.D. degrees from the University of California, Davis.

Dr. Looney has published a number of articles in professional journals and is the author of *The Economic Development of Iran, 1959–1981* (Praeger, 1973), *Income Distribution Policies and Economic Growth in Semi-Industrialized Countries: A Comparative Analysis of Iran, Mexico, Brazil, and South Korea* (Praeger, 1975), and *The Economic Development of Panama* (Praeger, 1976).